Southern Living

Christmas
Family Favorites
COOKBOOK

Southern Living®

Christmas
Family Favorites
C O O K B O O K

Oxmoor House®

LIBRARY OF CONGRESS CATALOG NUMBER: 00-130615

ISBN: 0-8487-1947-6

Printed in the United States of America

First Printing 2000

EDITOR-IN-CHIEF: Nancy Fitzpatrick Wyatt

SENIOR FOODS EDITOR: Susan Payne Stabler

SENIOR EDITOR, COPY AND HOMES: Olivia Kindig Wells

ART DIRECTOR: James Boone

Southern Living® *Christmas Family Favorites Cookbook*

EDITOR: Keri Bradford Anderson

COPY EDITOR: L. Amanda Owens

ASSOCIATE ART DIRECTOR: Cynthia R. Cooper

DESIGNER: Clare T. Minges

EDITORIAL ASSISTANT: Suzanne Powell

SENIOR PHOTOGRAPHERS: Jim Bathie, Sylvia Martin,
   Charles Walton IV

PHOTOGRAPHERS: Ralph Anderson, Tina Cornett, William Dickey,
   Brit Huckabay

SENIOR PHOTO STYLISTS: Cindy Manning Barr, Kay E. Clarke

PHOTO STYLISTS: Virginia R. Cravens, Mary Lynn Jenkins,
   Leslie Byars Simpson

DIRECTOR, PRODUCTION AND DISTRIBUTION: Phillip Lee

ASSOCIATE PRODUCTION MANAGER: Vanessa Cobbs Richardson

PRODUCTION ASSISTANT: Faye Porter Bonner

CONTRIBUTING INDEXER: Mary Ann Laurens

COVER: Italian Cream Cake (page 107)

BACK COVER: Wild Rice-Stuffed Turkey Breast (page 84),
   Roasted Winter Vegetables (page 97), Buttered Asparagus
   Spears (page 92)

PAGE 2: Beef Tenderloin with Five-Onion Sauce (page 70);
   Pistachio Risotto with Saffron (page 91); Oven-Roasted
   Potatoes, Green Beans, and Onions (page 96)

We're Here for You!

We at Oxmoor House are dedicated to serving you with
reliable information that expands your imagination and
enriches your life. We welcome your comments and sug-
gestions. Please write us at:

Oxmoor House, Inc.
Editor, *Southern Living*® *Christmas
   Family Favorites Cookbook*
2100 Lakeshore Drive
Birmingham, AL 35209

To order additional publications, call 1-205-877-6560.

.... ✦ ....

We Want Your Favorite Recipes!

Southern Living cooks are simply the best cooks, and we
want your secrets! Please send your favorite original
recipes and a sentence about why you like each one.
We can't guarantee we'll print them in a cookbook, but
if we do, we'll send you $20 and a free copy of the
cookbook. Send each recipe on a separate page, with
your name, address, and daytime phone number to:

Cookbook Recipes
Oxmoor House
2100 Lakeshore Drive
Birmingham, AL 35209

Contents

page 83

page 112

page 91

page 92

page 147

Festive Beginnings.................................7

Breakfast and Brunch Fare.................23

Christmas Breads.................35

Cozy Casual Entrées.................49

Entrées for the Feast.........................69

Seasonal Sides and Salads.................87

Classic Holiday Desserts.................105

Santa's Favorite
      Cookies and Candies.................125

Gifts from the Kitchen.................139

Special Occasion Menus.................149

Index.................156

Favorite Recipes Journal.................160

Festive Beginnings

*W*elcome family and friends to a Christmas celebration with these merry party-starters. ✦ Hosting a large crowd? No need to worry. Just prepare make-ahead recipes such as Savory Cheese Puffs (page 16), Sparkling Citrus Punch (page 21), and Southern Eggnog (page 21). Then relax and enjoy the festivities. ✦ Attending an informal holiday get-together? Follow Darlene Carroll's lead and serve a Pinecone Cheese Ball (page 12). It was such a hit the first time she served it at her family's annual Christmas Eve party that Darlene now brings it every year. ✦ Turn to these festive appetizers and beverages for all of your holiday parties, whether they are intimate or large, casual or elegant.

Christmas Crostini, page 13

Holiday Party Mix

For Charles and Mary White, the holidays are a time to renew family traditions. Each year they help their children give a Christmas party. Mary packages this party mix in festive bags so that no guest leaves empty-handed.

1 cup butter or margarine, melted
1 tablespoon Worcestershire sauce
1 teaspoon curry powder
½ teaspoon garlic salt
⅛ teaspoon hot sauce

6 cups corn chips
4 cups cheese crackers
3 cups mixed nuts
6 cups popped popcorn
1½ cups walnut pieces

✦ **Stir** together first 5 ingredients in a bowl. Combine corn chips and remaining 4 ingredients in a large roasting pan; add butter mixture, stirring to coat.
✦ **Bake** at 250° for 1 hour, stirring every 15 minutes. Spread on paper towels to cool. Store in an airtight container. **Yield:** 16 cups.

Mary White
Birmingham, Alabama

Sugar-and-Spice Pecans

¾ cup sugar
1 teaspoon ground cinnamon
½ teaspoon salt
¼ teaspoon ground nutmeg
¼ teaspoon ground allspice
¼ teaspoon ground cloves

1 egg white, lightly beaten
2½ tablespoons water
8 cups pecan halves
¾ teaspoon edible gold-leaf powder (optional)

✦ **Stir** together first 8 ingredients in a bowl. Add pecans; stir until coated. Spread in a lightly greased, aluminum foil-lined 15- x 10-inch jellyroll pan.
✦ **Bake** at 275° for 50 minutes, stirring occasionally. Remove from pan; cool on wax paper. Place in a heavy-duty, zip-top plastic bag; if desired, sprinkle with gold-leaf powder, shaking to coat. Store in an airtight container. **Yield:** 8 cups.

Note: You can find edible gold-leaf powder at most cooking specialty stores.

Sweet-and-Spicy Mustard Dip

3 tablespoons mayonnaise
3 tablespoons coarse-grained Dijon mustard

1 tablespoon prepared horseradish
2 teaspoons sugar

✦ **Stir** together all ingredients in a 1-cup liquid measuring cup; microwave at HIGH 30 seconds, stirring once. Serve with chicken fingers. **Yield:** ⅓ cup.

Charlene Barton
Dora, Alabama

Layered Nacho Dip

This family favorite is so simple, yet so divine. Serve it with red and green tortilla chips to carry out the holiday theme.

2 (16-ounce) cans refried beans
1 (4.5-ounce) can chopped green
   chiles, undrained
1 (1¼-ounce) package taco
   seasoning mix
1 (8-ounce) package shredded
   Mexican cheese blend

1 (8-ounce) container refrigerated
   avocado dip
1 (8-ounce) carton sour cream
3 green onions, thinly sliced
2 (2¼-ounce) cans sliced ripe olives,
   drained
1 large tomato, chopped

✦ **Stir** together first 3 ingredients; spread into an 11- x 7-inch baking dish.
✦ **Bake** at 350° for 25 minutes or until thoroughly heated. Sprinkle evenly
with cheese; bake 5 more minutes or until cheese melts.
✦ **Spread** avocado dip over cheese; spread sour cream over avocado dip. Top
evenly with green onions, olives, and tomato. Serve warm with tortilla chips or
corn chips. **Yield:** 10 servings.

Note: If you're in a hurry, heat this dip in your microwave oven. Cook bean
mixture at HIGH 3 to 4 minutes or until heated. Top with cheese; cook at
HIGH 2 more minutes or until cheese melts. Proceed with recipe as directed.

Spinach Dip in Sourdough Round

*Always a crowd-pleaser, this dip goes nicely with sourdough
bread for a winning flavor combination.*

1 (10-ounce) package frozen chopped
    spinach, thawed
4 green onions, chopped
2 cups mayonnaise
½ teaspoon lemon juice

½ teaspoon Worcestershire sauce
1 teaspoon garlic powder
1 teaspoon seasoned salt
2 (16-ounce) round sourdough loaves

✦ **Drain** spinach well, pressing between layers of paper towels to remove
excess moisture.

✦ **Stir** together spinach, green onions, and next 5 ingredients; cover and chill
at least 2 hours.

✦ **Cut** 1 bread loaf into cubes; set aside.

✦ **Hollow** out remaining loaf, leaving a 1-inch-thick shell; spoon dip into shell.
Serve with bread cubes and assorted raw vegetables. **Yield:** 2½ cups.

Grandma Reed's Seafood Spread

*Mississippi native
Melissa Reed
Youngblood would
never consider relin-
quishing generations
of Southern traditions,
even though she no
longer lives in the
South. Here is one of
her most treasured
heirlooms—a recipe
from her grandmother.
Make it part of your
recipe collection.*

5 cups water
1½ pounds unpeeled medium-size
    fresh shrimp
½ pound fresh lump crabmeat,
    drained
1 (8-ounce) package cream cheese,
    softened
2 tablespoons mayonnaise

1 tablespoon lemon juice
1 teaspoon Worcestershire sauce
½ teaspoon hot sauce
¼ teaspoon salt
¼ teaspoon pepper
3 green onions, thinly sliced
Garnish: fresh dill sprigs

✦ **Bring** 5 cups water to a boil in a medium saucepan; add shrimp, and cook
3 to 5 minutes or just until shrimp turn pink. Drain and rinse with cold water.
Peel shrimp; devein, if desired. Chop shrimp.

✦ **Stir** together shrimp, crabmeat, and next 8 ingredients; cover and chill up to
24 hours. Serve on cucumber slices and squash slices or in phyllo cups.
Garnish, if desired. **Yield:** 5 cups.

*Melissa Reed Youngblood
Summit, New Jersey*

Feta Cheese Spread

2 (4-ounce) packages crumbled feta
  cheese
1 (8-ounce) package reduced-fat
  cream cheese, softened
2 tablespoons fat-free milk

10 fresh mint leaves
1 or 2 garlic cloves
Garnishes: chopped tomato, cucumber,
  green onions

◆ **Process** first 5 ingredients in a food processor until smooth. Transfer to a serving bowl. Serve immediately, or cover and chill. Serve spread with toasted baguette slices and assorted fresh vegetables. Garnish, if desired. **Yield:** 2 cups.

Paula Covault
LaGrange, Kentucky

Paula Covault created this simple, savory spread with a key ingredient in mind. "My husband is Greek and loves feta cheese, so I'm always looking for ways to use it," she explains.

Roasted Red Bell Pepper Spread

This recipe yields a lot of spread; serve the leftovers
on pasta and grilled fish or chicken.

4 large red bell peppers
1 (8-ounce) package sliced fresh
  mushrooms
¼ cup chopped purple onion
2 garlic cloves, minced
2 tablespoons olive oil, divided
1 cup grated Parmesan cheese
½ cup Italian-seasoned breadcrumbs
¼ cup walnut pieces, toasted and
  finely chopped

2 tablespoons minced fresh basil or
  2 teaspoons dried basil
2 teaspoons lemon juice
1 teaspoon Worcestershire sauce
¼ teaspoon salt
¼ teaspoon pepper
¼ teaspoon hot sauce
Garnish: fresh basil leaves

◆ **Place** bell peppers on an aluminum foil-lined baking sheet.
◆ **Broil** 5 inches from heat (with electric oven door partially open) 5 to 10 minutes on each side or until bell peppers look blistered.
◆ **Place** bell peppers in a heavy-duty, zip-top plastic bag; seal and let stand 10 minutes to loosen skins. Peel bell peppers; remove and discard seeds.
◆ **Sauté** mushrooms, onion, and garlic in 1½ teaspoons hot oil in a large skillet 10 minutes or until liquid evaporates. Remove from heat.
◆ **Process** bell peppers in a food processor until smooth, stopping to scrape down sides. Add mushroom mixture, remaining 1½ tablespoons oil, cheese, and next 8 ingredients; pulse until ground.
◆ **Serve** with breadsticks, crackers, or assorted fresh vegetables. Garnish, if desired. **Yield:** 3 cups.

Patricia Agnew
Charleston, South Carolina

Pinecone Cheese Ball

*Darlene chose pecans for her striking cheese ball
because they make a more realistic-looking pinecone than almonds do.*

1 (8-ounce) container garden
   vegetable cream cheese
1 (8-ounce) container roasted garlic
   cream cheese
1 cup (4 ounces) shredded sharp
   Cheddar cheese

3 green onions, chopped
2 cups pecan halves, toasted
Fresh rosemary sprigs

◆ **Stir** together first 4 ingredients. Shape into an oval; cover and chill 2 hours.

◆ **Arrange** pecan halves over cheese oval in overlapping rows, beginning at
bottom and working upward, to resemble a pinecone. Arrange rosemary sprigs
at top of pinecone. Serve with assorted crackers. **Yield:** 16 servings.

*Darlene Carroll
Londonderry, Ohio*

Showstopping Appetizer Torte

1½ cups chopped pecans
4 (8-ounce) packages cream cheese, softened and divided
3 tablespoons mustard-mayonnaise sauce, divided
½ cup chopped green onions
1 (8-ounce) package shredded sharp Cheddar cheese
1 (7-ounce) can crushed pineapple, drained
2 teaspoons dried mint
1¼ cups orange marmalade, divided
1 tablespoon mayonnaise
2 tablespoons dried orange peel
2 to 3 teaspoons orange extract
Garnish: toasted pecan halves

✦ **Bake** chopped pecans in a shallow pan at 350° for 5 to 10 minutes or until lightly toasted, stirring occasionally. Remove from pan, and set aside.

✦ **Process** 2 packages cream cheese, 2 tablespoons mustard-mayonnaise sauce, and next 4 ingredients in a food processor until blended, stopping to scrape down sides. Press into bottom of a plastic wrap-lined 9-inch springform pan. Sprinkle with chopped pecans.

✦ **Process** remaining 2 packages cream cheese, remaining 1 tablespoon mustard-mayonnaise sauce, ⅔ cup orange marmalade, and next 3 ingredients in food processor until smooth, stopping to scrape down sides.

✦ **Spread** mixture over torte, pressing until smooth. Cover and chill up to 3 days. Remove from pan; spread with remaining marmalade. Garnish, if desired. Serve with gingersnaps. **Yield:** about 30 appetizer servings.

Raleigh McDonald Hussung
Brentwood, Tennessee

"This is a truly festive holiday showstopping appetizer, the one I begin every holiday party with. It's wonderful because I can make it ahead, and it will serve a crowd. Accompanied by the gingersnaps, it will bring raves!"
—Raleigh McDonald Hussung

Christmas Crostini

(pictured on page 6)

1 French baguette
1 (8-ounce) package cream cheese, softened
½ cup (2 ounces) shredded Swiss cheese
½ cup mayonnaise or salad dressing
1 (0.7-ounce) package Italian dressing mix
Garnishes: quartered cucumber slices, chopped red bell pepper, toasted almond slices, chopped green onions

✦ **Slice** baguette into 36 (¼- to ½-inch) slices; place, cut side down, on an aluminum foil-lined baking sheet.

✦ **Bake** at 400° for 5 minutes or until lightly browned.

✦ **Combine** cream cheese and next 3 ingredients; spread on bread slices.

✦ **Bake** at 400° for 5 minutes or until cheese melts. Garnish, if desired. Serve immediately. **Yield:** 3 dozen.

Maia L. Artman
Norman, Oklahoma

Pear-Pecan Appetizers

1 cup finely chopped pecans
2 ripe pears
1 quart water
2 tablespoons lemon juice

½ cup butter or margarine,
    softened
2 tablespoons crumbled blue cheese

✦ **Bake** pecans in a shallow pan at 350° for 5 to 10 minutes or until toasted, stirring occasionally. Set aside.

✦ **Cut** each pear into thin slices, leaving stems intact, if desired. Combine pear slices, water, and lemon juice in a large bowl.

✦ **Beat** butter and blue cheese at medium speed with an electric mixer until smooth.

✦ **Drain** pear slices on paper towels. Spread bottom half of pear slices with butter mixture; coat with pecans, and place on a serving plate. Cover and chill 30 minutes. **Yield:** 2½ dozen.

Marinated Shrimp

2½ quarts water
3 pounds unpeeled medium-size fresh shrimp
2 small green bell peppers
2 medium onions
2 cups white vinegar

1½ cups ketchup
½ cup vegetable oil
1 tablespoon celery seeds
1½ tablespoons Worcestershire sauce
1 teaspoon hot sauce

✦ **Bring** 2½ quarts water to a boil; add shrimp, and cook 3 to 5 minutes or just until shrimp turn pink. Drain and rinse with cold water. Peel shrimp; devein, if desired.

✦ **Cut** peppers and onions into strips. Place in a shallow dish or heavy-duty, zip-top plastic bag; add shrimp.

✦ **Stir** together vinegar and remaining 5 ingredients in a small bowl; pour over shrimp mixture. Cover dish, or seal bag; chill 8 hours, turning occasionally. **Yield:** 8 appetizer servings.

Denise Bagnall
Ashland, Virginia

Red Wine-Marinated Flank Steak

1 cup reduced-calorie Italian dressing
⅔ cup soy sauce
⅔ cup dry red wine
⅓ cup sliced green onions
1 teaspoon dry mustard

¼ teaspoon lemon-pepper seasoning
2 garlic cloves, minced
1 lemon, thinly sliced
2 (1½-pound) flank steaks

✦ **Combine** first 8 ingredients in a large shallow dish or heavy-duty, zip-top plastic bag; add steaks, turning to coat. Cover dish, or seal bag; chill 8 to 12 hours, turning steaks occasionally.

✦ **Remove** steaks from marinade, and discard marinade. Place steaks on a lightly greased rack in a broiler pan.

✦ **Broil** 3 inches from heat (with electric oven door partially open) 7 to 10 minutes on each side or to desired degree of doneness. Thinly slice steaks diagonally across grain. Serve warm or chilled with biscuits and coarse-grained Dijon mustard. **Yield:** 24 appetizer servings.

Mildred Bickley
Bristol, Virginia

> ✦
>
> *"I've had this wine-marinated steak recipe for so long—I think it actually came from my mother. I serve it probably twice a month, either in biscuits for a party or sliced as a main dish for the family."*
> *—Mildred Bickley*

Savory Cheese Puffs

Betty Lawandales
likes to serve these
buttery cheese puffs at
her neighborhood's
annual progressive
appetizer party.
They're great for
Christmas parties
because they can be
made up to two weeks
ahead.

2 large eggs
1 (3-ounce) package cream cheese, softened
¼ cup cottage cheese
4 ounces crumbled feta cheese
1 (16-ounce) package frozen phyllo pastry, thawed
Unsalted butter, melted

✦ **Beat** eggs at medium speed with an electric mixer 1 minute; beat in cheeses.
✦ **Unfold** phyllo; cover with a damp towel. Place 1 phyllo sheet on a flat surface covered with wax paper; cut into 3 (12- x 6-inch) strips. Brush 1 long side of strips with butter. Fold strips in half lengthwise; brush with butter. Spoon 1 teaspoon cheese mixture onto base of each strip; fold right bottom corner over to form a triangle. Fold back and forth into a triangle, gently pressing corners together. Place triangles, seam side down, on ungreased baking sheets; brush with butter. Repeat procedure with remaining phyllo, cheese mixture, and butter. Bake at 375° for 15 minutes or until golden. (If desired, freeze unbaked pastries on baking sheets; then place in airtight containers. Store in freezer up to 2 weeks. Bake as directed without thawing.) **Yield:** 5¼ dozen.

Betty Lawandales
Charleston, South Carolina

Hot Phyllo Burritos

8 green onions
1¾ cups salsa, divided
1 (16-ounce) can pinto beans, rinsed and drained
1 jalapeño pepper, halved
1 (1¼-ounce) package taco seasoning mix
1 (16-ounce) package frozen phyllo pastry, thawed

✦ **Cut** green tops from onions. Cook tops in boiling water to cover 1 minute. Plunge into ice water; drain. Cut each piece lengthwise into 3 or 4 strips. Chop enough of white portions of onions to measure ½ cup; process chopped onion, 2 teaspoons salsa, and next 3 ingredients in a food processor until smooth.
✦ **Place** 1 phyllo sheet on a large cutting board; coat with cooking spray. Keep remaining phyllo covered with a damp towel. Stack 3 more phyllo sheets over first, coating each with cooking spray. Cut stack in half lengthwise; cut each half crosswise into thirds. Spoon 1 tablespoon bean mixture near 1 long edge of each stack; roll up, starting at same edge. Pinch rolls 1½ inches from each end; tie with green onion strips. Place on greased baking sheets. Repeat procedure 3 times. (Reserve any remaining phyllo for another use.) Bake burritos at 400° for 10 to 15 minutes or until golden; cool on wire racks. Serve with remaining salsa. **Yield:** 2 dozen.

Judy Carter
Winchester, Tennessee

Tortellini Tapas with Spicy Ranch Dip

1 (9-ounce) package refrigerated
    cheese-filled tortellini
1 (16-ounce) bottle Ranch-style
    dressing with peppercorns*
2 large eggs

2 cups fine, dry breadcrumbs
¾ cup mild chunky salsa
¼ cup chopped fresh cilantro
2 cups vegetable oil
Garnish: fresh cilantro sprigs

✦ **Cook** tortellini according to package directions; drain and cool. Whisk together 1 cup dressing and eggs in a large bowl until blended.
✦ **Add** tortellini, and let stand 10 minutes. Drain and dredge in breadcrumbs; place on a baking sheet. Cover and chill at least 1 hour. Stir together remaining dressing, salsa, and chopped cilantro; cover dip, and chill.
✦ **Pour** oil into a Dutch oven; heat to 375°. Fry tortellini, in batches, until golden. Drain on paper towels. Garnish, if desired. Serve with dip. **Yield:** 8 appetizer servings.

* Substitute 1 (16-ounce) bottle Ranch-style dressing plus ½ teaspoon cracked black pepper, if desired.

Note: To make ahead, fry tortellini according to directions; drain and place on a baking sheet. Keep warm in a 200° oven up to 2 hours.

Loanne Chiu
Fort Worth, Texas

"Tortellini have always reminded me of miniature Chinese wontons, so I decided to try frying them," Loanne Chiu says. "It was a mix and match of tastes and cooking techniques."

Loanne says that her first version of Tortellini Tapas was "hard and inedible," so she kept testing. "The breadcrumb coating was the key," she discovered. "It allowed the tortellini to stay tender."

Sweet-and-Sour Meatballs

1 (20-ounce) package frozen
    Italian-style meatballs
1 (12-ounce) bottle chili sauce

1 (10-ounce) jar grape jelly
1 (8-ounce) can pineapple chunks,
    drained (optional)

✦ **Cook** meatballs in a large nonstick skillet over medium heat 4 minutes or until browned. Drain meatballs, and return to skillet.

✦ **Add** chili sauce and jelly, and cook until jelly melts, stirring constantly. Add pineapple, if desired. Bring to a boil; reduce heat, and simmer 10 minutes, stirring occasionally. **Yield:** 12 appetizer servings.

Note: For a speedy and spicy entrée that will serve four, spoon these meatballs over hot cooked rice.

Sticky Chicken

*A coating of soy and teriyaki sauces flavors
these wings, which rival any you find in restaurants.*

2 pounds chicken wings (about 16
    wings)
3/4 cup soy sauce
1/2 cup teriyaki sauce

1/2 cup butter or margarine, melted
1 cup firmly packed light brown sugar
1 tablespoon Creole seasoning
1 teaspoon dry mustard

✦ **Cut** off and discard chicken wingtips; cut wings in half at joint (kitchen scissors work well).

✦ **Combine** soy sauce and remaining 5 ingredients in a large heavy-duty, zip-top plastic bag.

✦ **Add** chicken pieces to soy sauce mixture. Seal bag, and squeeze bag to coat chicken; chill 1 hour.

✦ **Line** a roasting pan with aluminum foil; coat foil with vegetable cooking spray. Drain chicken, and discard marinade. Place chicken in pan.

✦ **Bake** chicken at 375° for 40 minutes or until browned. Serve with carrot sticks, celery sticks, and Ranch-style or blue cheese dressing, if desired. **Yield:** 4 appetizer servings.

Catherine W. McCrary
Woodstock, Georgia

Hot Russian Tea

4 quarts water, divided
1 cup sugar
4 (2-inch) cinnamon sticks
2 (12-ounce) cans frozen pineapple-orange-banana juice concentrate, undiluted
1 (12-ounce) can frozen lemonade concentrate, undiluted
⅓ cup unsweetened instant tea powder
Garnish: orange slices

✦ **Bring** 1 quart water, sugar, and cinnamon sticks to a boil in a Dutch oven over medium-high heat, stirring until sugar dissolves.
✦ **Stir** in remaining 3 quarts water, fruit concentrates, and tea powder.
✦ **Cook** until thoroughly heated. Garnish, if desired. Serve immediately. **Yield:** 20 cups.

Lea Snell
Florence, Alabama

When Lea Snell began hosting a mother-daughter Christmas tea, the girls brought baby dolls to the party. Now, they're in junior high, but they still look forward to the annual event, at which they always enjoy this tea and assorted cookies.

Hot Chocolate

4 cups milk
¾ cup semisweet chocolate morsels
1 teaspoon vanilla extract
½ cup miniature marshmallows

✦ **Combine** milk and chocolate morsels in a heavy 2-quart saucepan; cook over low heat, stirring constantly, until chocolate melts. Stir in vanilla.
✦ **Pour** into mugs; sprinkle with marshmallows. **Yield:** 4 cups.

Praline Coffee

3 cups hot brewed coffee
¾ cup half-and-half
¾ cup firmly packed light brown sugar
2 tablespoons butter
¾ cup praline liqueur
Sweetened whipped cream

✦ **Cook** first 4 ingredients in a large saucepan over medium heat, stirring constantly, until thoroughly heated (do not boil).
✦ **Stir** in liqueur; top with sweetened whipped cream. **Yield:** about 6 cups.

Paula McCollum
Springtown, Texas

Spiced Cranberry Cider

This ruby red cider pairs perfectly with another of Marty Wingate's specialties, Brown Sugar Shortbread (see page 130).

1 quart apple cider
3 cups cranberry juice drink
2 to 3 tablespoons brown sugar
¾ teaspoon whole cloves

2 (3-inch) cinnamon sticks
½ lemon, thinly sliced
Garnish: cinnamon sticks

✦ **Bring** first 6 ingredients to a boil in a Dutch oven, stirring often; reduce heat, and simmer, uncovered, 15 to 20 minutes. Discard spices and lemon. Garnish, if desired. **Yield:** 7 cups.

Marty Wingate
Seattle, Washington

Spiced
Cranberry Cider

Brown Sugar
Shortbread, page 130

Sparkling Citrus Punch

1 (46-ounce) can pineapple juice
1½ cups orange juice
¾ cup lemon juice
¼ cup lime juice
1¼ cups sugar
2 (2-liter) bottles ginger ale, chilled

✦ **Stir** together first 5 ingredients until sugar dissolves. Pour into ice cube trays. Cover and freeze until firm. To serve, place 4 juice cubes in each tall glass. Pour 1 cup ginger ale into each glass; stir until slushy. **Yield:** about 17 servings.

Note: Freeze juice mixture in an airtight container, if desired. Thaw slightly in a punch bowl; add ginger ale, and stir until slushy.

Julia Garmon
Colonial Beach, Virginia

Lemonade-Bourbon Punch

Chilling the ingredients before mixing them together allows this beverage to be icy cold and ready to serve as soon as you make it.

2 (6-ounce) cans frozen lemonade concentrate, thawed and undiluted
1¾ cups orange juice, chilled
¾ cup lemon juice, chilled
1 (2-liter) bottle lemon-lime carbonated beverage, chilled
1 quart club soda, chilled
1 pint bourbon, chilled

✦ **Stir** together first 3 ingredients in a punch bowl. Slowly stir in lemon-lime beverage, club soda, and bourbon. Serve over ice, if desired. **Yield:** 18 cups.

Molly Ellis
Clarksville, Tennessee

> ....✦..............
> *"Punch is just part of the holidays for me. I make two batches and leave the bourbon out of one so that the children can have their own festive drink."*
> —*Molly Ellis*

Southern Eggnog

2 quarts milk, divided
12 large eggs, lightly beaten
1½ cups sugar
½ teaspoon salt
2 tablespoons vanilla extract
1 teaspoon ground nutmeg
1 cup bourbon
2 cups whipping cream, whipped

✦ **Stir** together 1 quart milk, eggs, sugar, and salt in a large saucepan. Cook over low heat, stirring constantly, about 25 minutes or until mixture thickens and coats back of a spoon (do not boil).
✦ **Stir** in remaining milk, vanilla, and nutmeg. Pour into a large bowl; stir in bourbon. Cover and chill thoroughly. Just before serving, fold in whipped cream. Transfer to a large punch bowl. **Yield:** 15 cups.

Breakfast and Brunch Fare

Count on these delicious eye-openers as part of your holidays, whether you're hosting a hearty brunch for a crowd or a cozy Christmas breakfast at home. ✦ Make-ahead recipes, such as Sausage-Filled Crêpes (page 26) and Christmas Morning Sticky Buns (page 33), make for uncomplicated mornings. Prepare them ahead of time—then open presents with your family while your oven does all the work. ✦ Treat out-of-town guests to a memorable brunch with impressive Southwestern Soufflé Roll (page 24) or hearty Eggs Oso Grande (page 25). These inviting recipes are perfect wake-up calls.

Southwestern Soufflé Roll, page 24

Southwestern Soufflé Roll

(pictured on page 22)

(pictured on page 22)

Lilann Taylor's hearty egg dish is a refreshing alternative to a breakfast casserole. Serve it with orange slices, strawberries, and starfruit, and you'll have an impressive morning meal for holiday guests.

Save time by chopping the peppers, onion, garlic, and ham the day before; then store in separate zip-top plastic bags in the refrigerator. Make the Salsa the day before, or use your favorite store-bought salsa instead.

2 tablespoons butter or margarine
1½ cups peeled, diced potato
2 green bell peppers, chopped
1 onion, chopped
2 jalapeño peppers, seeded and minced
4 garlic cloves, minced
4 ounces ham, diced
½ cup chopped fresh cilantro
½ teaspoon salt
¼ teaspoon pepper
¼ cup butter or margarine, melted
2 tablespoons all-purpose flour
¼ teaspoon salt
1 cup milk
12 large eggs, separated
1 cup (4 ounces) shredded Monterey Jack cheese with peppers
Salsa

✦ **Melt** 2 tablespoons butter in a skillet; add potato and next 4 ingredients. Sauté 20 minutes or until tender. Stir in ham and next 3 ingredients; set aside.

✦ **Whisk** together ¼ cup melted butter, flour, and ¼ teaspoon salt in a heavy saucepan over low heat until smooth; cook, whisking constantly, 3 minutes or until bubbly. Gradually add milk, and cook over medium heat, whisking constantly, until thickened and bubbly. Remove from heat.

✦ **Beat** egg yolks until thick and pale. Gradually stir about one-fourth of milk mixture into yolks; add to remaining milk mixture, stirring constantly.

✦ **Cook** over medium-low heat, stirring constantly, 2 minutes or until slightly thickened. Pour batter into a large bowl, and cool.

✦ **Line** a 15- x 10-inch jellyroll pan with parchment paper; lightly coat paper with vegetable cooking spray. Beat egg whites at high speed with an electric mixer until stiff peaks form; fold into batter. Spread evenly in prepared pan.

✦ **Bake** at 400° for 15 minutes or until a wooden pick inserted in center comes out clean. Cool in pan on a wire rack 5 minutes. Turn out onto a cloth towel; remove paper. Return paper to pan. Top soufflé with vegetable mixture; sprinkle with cheese. Beginning at a long side, roll up, jellyroll fashion; place roll, seam side down, in pan. Bake at 350° for 10 minutes or until heated and cheese melts. Slice with a serrated knife; serve with Salsa. **Yield:** 8 servings.

Salsa

2 cups diced fresh tomato
¼ cup chopped onion
¼ cup chopped fresh cilantro
2 tablespoons lime juice
½ teaspoon salt
½ teaspoon pepper
2 jalapeño peppers, seeded and minced

✦ **Combine** all ingredients in a bowl; cover and chill. **Yield:** 2¼ cups.

Lilann Taylor
Savannah, Georgia

Eggs Oso Grande

1 (9-ounce) package frozen creamed
   spinach
3 ripe plum tomatoes
½ teaspoon dried oregano
½ teaspoon dried basil
2 tablespoons butter or margarine
2 tablespoons grated Parmesan cheese

4 large eggs
2 English muffins, split and toasted
¼ teaspoon salt
¼ teaspoon pepper
Freshly grated Parmesan cheese
6 bacon slices, cooked and crumbled

✦ **Cook** spinach according to package directions; keep warm. Cut tomatoes
into ¼-inch-thick slices; place in a 15- x 10-inch jellyroll pan. Sprinkle with
oregano and basil; dot with butter. Sprinkle with 2 tablespoons cheese. Broil
5 inches from heat (with electric oven door partially open) 2 minutes.
✦ **Bring** 2 inches of water to a boil in a large saucepan; reduce heat to main-
tain a simmer. Break 1 egg into a saucer; slip egg into water, holding saucer
close to water surface. Repeat procedure with remaining 3 eggs. Simmer
5 minutes or until done. Remove with a slotted spoon; trim edges, if desired.
✦ **Top** muffin halves with tomato. Place eggs over tomato; sprinkle with salt
and pepper. Top with spinach, and sprinkle with cheese. Top with bacon; serve
immediately with your favorite fresh fruit. **Yield:** 2 servings.

Nan Rowe
Pagosa Springs, Colorado

*This filling breakfast
gets its name from the
Rocky Mountain ranch
that former Southerner
Nan Rowe and her
husband, Gary,
run—Oso Grande
(Big Bear) Ranch.
Great food such as
this, along with a
strong dose of Nan's
Southern hospitality,
keeps folks returning.
Enjoy her delectable
recipe for a taste of
the holidays from the
ranch.*

Country Ham with Redeye Gravy

2 cups hot strong brewed coffee
¼ cup firmly packed brown sugar

2 (12-ounce) slices boneless country ham

✦ **Stir** together coffee and sugar; cool.
✦ **Cook** ham in a large cast-iron skillet over medium heat 5 to 7 minutes on each side or until browned. Remove ham; keep warm, reserving drippings in skillet.
✦ **Add** coffee mixture to skillet, stirring to loosen particles from bottom; bring to a boil. Boil, stirring occasionally, until reduced by half (about 15 minutes). Serve immediately with ham. **Yield:** 6 servings.

Roevis McKay
New York, New York

Sausage-Filled Crêpes

1 pound ground pork sausage
1 small onion, diced
2 cups (8 ounces) shredded Cheddar cheese, divided
1 (3-ounce) package cream cheese
½ teaspoon dried marjoram

Basic Crêpes
½ cup sour cream
¼ cup butter or margarine, softened
¼ cup chopped fresh parsley

✦ **Cook** sausage and onion in a skillet over medium heat, stirring until sausage crumbles and is no longer pink; drain. Return to skillet. Add 1 cup Cheddar cheese, cream cheese, and marjoram, stirring until cheeses melt. Spoon 3 tablespoons filling down center of each Basic Crêpe.
✦ **Roll** up; place, seam side down, in a lightly greased 13- x 9-inch baking dish.
✦ **Bake,** covered, at 350° for 15 minutes. Combine sour cream and butter; spoon over crêpes. Bake 5 minutes. Sprinkle with remaining 1 cup Cheddar cheese and parsley. Serve with sliced tomato. **Yield:** 6 to 8 servings.

Basic Crêpes

3 large eggs
1 cup milk
1 tablespoon vegetable oil

1 cup all-purpose flour
½ teaspoon salt

✦ **Beat** first 3 ingredients at medium speed with an electric mixer until mixture is blended. Gradually add flour and salt, beating until smooth. Cover and chill 1 hour.
✦ **Coat** bottom of a 7-inch nonstick skillet with vegetable cooking spray; place skillet over medium heat until hot. Pour 3 tablespoons batter into skillet, and quickly tilt in all directions so that batter covers bottom of skillet.

✦ **Cook** 1 minute or until crêpe can be shaken loose from skillet. Turn crêpe over, and cook about 30 seconds. Place on a cloth towel to cool. Repeat procedure with remaining batter. Stack crêpes between sheets of wax paper. **Yield:** 12 (7-inch) crêpes.

Note: Assemble Sausage-Filled Crêpes ahead, if desired, and freeze. To reheat, remove from freezer; let stand 30 minutes at room temperature. Bake, covered, at 350° for 40 minutes or until thoroughly heated. Proceed as directed, adding sour cream topping and remaining ingredients.

Beth Ann Stein
Apple Valley, Minnesota

Egg Casserole

6 cups cubed cooked ham
4 cups (16 ounces) shredded Cheddar
   cheese
8 cups French bread cubes
3 tablespoons butter, melted

½ cup all-purpose flour
1 teaspoon dry mustard
8 large eggs
4 cups milk

+ **Layer** ham, cheese, and bread in a lightly greased 13- x 9-inch baking dish; drizzle with butter. Stir together flour and mustard; sprinkle over casserole. Whisk together eggs and milk; pour over casserole. Cover and chill 8 hours.
+ **Remove** from refrigerator; let stand at room temperature 15 minutes.
+ **Bake** at 350° for 50 to 55 minutes or until set. **Yield:** 8 to 10 servings.

Ginny Munsterman
Garland, Texas

Garlic-Cheese Grits

(pictured on page 152)

These grits from Beth Ann Spracklen are ideal for a brunch buffet because they will serve a crowd. You can easily halve the recipe to serve fewer people.

3½ quarts water
1½ tablespoons salt
4 cups uncooked quick-cooking grits
5 garlic cloves, minced

1 (2-pound) loaf process cheese
   spread, cubed
1 cup half-and-half
⅔ cup butter or margarine

+ **Bring** water and salt to a boil in a large Dutch oven; gradually stir in grits and garlic. Cover, reduce heat, and simmer 10 minutes, stirring occasionally.
+ **Add** cheese, half-and-half, and butter; simmer, stirring constantly, until cheese and butter melt. **Yield:** 36 servings.

Beth Ann Spracklen
Arlington, Texas

Hash Brown-Cheese Bake

1 (20-ounce) package refrigerated
   shredded hash browns
1 (10¾-ounce) can cream of celery
   soup, undiluted
1 (8-ounce) container sour cream

1 (2-ounce) jar diced pimiento,
   drained
½ cup grated Parmesan cheese
1 cup (4 ounces) shredded sharp
   Cheddar cheese, divided

+ **Stir** together first 5 ingredients and ½ cup shredded Cheddar cheese; spoon mixture into a lightly greased 13- x 9-inch baking dish.
+ **Bake,** uncovered, at 350° for 40 minutes. Sprinkle with remaining ½ cup Cheddar cheese, and bake 5 more minutes. **Yield:** 6 to 8 servings.

Citrus Compote with Caramel Syrup

¾ cup sugar
¾ cup cold water, divided
¼ cup light corn syrup
¼ teaspoon ground cinnamon
⅛ teaspoon ground cloves

5 large naval oranges, peeled and
    sectioned*
4 pink grapefruit, peeled and
    sectioned*

✦ **Cook** sugar, ¼ cup cold water, and syrup in a heavy saucepan over medium heat, stirring constantly, 30 minutes or until caramel colored. Remove from heat. Add remaining ½ cup water. (Sugar mixture will clump but will dissolve when heated.) Bring to a boil.

✦ **Boil,** stirring constantly, 5 minutes or until smooth. Stir in cinnamon and cloves. Pour over fruit. Serve warm. **Yield:** 6 servings.

* Substitute 3⅓ cups jarred orange sections, drained, and 5 cups jarred grapefruit sections, drained, for fresh oranges and grapefruit, if desired.

Note: Make syrup ahead, if desired, and chill. Reheat before serving over fruit.

Brandied Fruit Compote

Get a head start on holiday cooking with this versatile spiced dried-fruit medley.
The flavors blend and improve as the dish chills.

¾ cup pitted prunes
½ cup dried apricot halves
½ cup dried apple slices
5 dried figs
1 orange
1 cup dried cranberries
½ cup dried cherries
½ cup flaked coconut

¼ cup raisins
¼ cup golden raisins
1 cup brandy, divided
½ cup honey
½ teaspoon ground cinnamon
¼ teaspoon ground cloves
2 cups water
¾ cup sugar

✦ **Place** first 4 ingredients in a bowl. Peel orange with a vegetable peeler, reserving sections for another use. Cut rind into very thin strips; stir rind, cranberries, and next 4 ingredients into prune mixture.

✦ **Stir** together ½ cup brandy and next 3 ingredients in a heavy saucepan; cook over medium heat 3 minutes or until warm. Gently stir in fruit mixture.

✦ **Stir** in 2 cups water, sugar, and remaining ½ cup brandy. Cook over low heat 15 minutes, stirring occasionally; cool. Cover and store in refrigerator up to 1 month; serve at room temperature. **Yield:** 5 cups.

Raspberry-Cheese Coffee Cake

1 (8-ounce) package cream cheese,
    softened
½ cup butter or margarine, softened
1 cup sugar
¼ cup milk
½ teaspoon vanilla extract
2 large eggs

1¾ cups all-purpose flour
1 teaspoon baking powder
½ teaspoon baking soda
¼ teaspoon salt
½ cup seedless raspberry preserves
3 tablespoons powdered sugar

✦ **Beat** first 3 ingredients at medium speed with an electric mixer until creamy. Add milk, vanilla, and eggs, beating until smooth.

✦ **Stir** together flour and next 3 ingredients; add to cream cheese mixture, beating at low speed until well blended.

✦ **Spread** batter into a greased and floured 13- x 9-inch pan. Dollop with preserves, and swirl with a knife.

✦ **Bake** at 350° for 30 minutes or until cake begins to leave sides of pan. Cool slightly, and sprinkle with powdered sugar. Cut into squares. **Yield:** 12 to 15 servings.

Clarice Lowery
Rockwell, North Carolina

Biscuits and Sausage Gravy

(pictured on page 152)

3 cups self-rising soft wheat flour
¼ teaspoon baking soda
1 teaspoon sugar
½ cup butter-flavored shortening

1¼ cups buttermilk
Butter or margarine, melted
Sausage Gravy

✦ **Stir** together first 3 ingredients in a large bowl; cut in shortening with a pastry blender until mixture is crumbly.

✦ **Add** buttermilk, stirring just until dry ingredients are moistened. Turn dough out onto a lightly floured surface; knead 4 or 5 times.

✦ **Roll** dough to ¾-inch thickness; cut with a 2½-inch biscuit cutter. Place on a lightly greased baking sheet. Bake at 425° for 12 minutes or until golden. Brush tops with butter. Split biscuits open; serve with Sausage Gravy. **Yield:** 12 to 14 servings.

Sausage Gravy

½ pound ground pork sausage
¼ cup butter or margarine
⅓ cup all-purpose flour
3¼ cups low-fat or whole milk

½ teaspoon salt
½ teaspoon pepper
⅛ teaspoon dried Italian seasoning

✦ **Brown** sausage in a skillet, stirring until it crumbles. Drain, reserving 1 tablespoon drippings in skillet. Set sausage aside.

✦ **Add** butter to drippings; heat over low heat until butter melts. Add flour, stirring until smooth.

✦ **Cook,** stirring constantly, 1 minute. Gradually add milk; cook over medium heat, stirring constantly, until thickened and bubbly. Stir in seasonings and sausage. Cook, stirring constantly, until thoroughly heated. **Yield:** 3¾ cups.

Diane Hogan
Birmingham, Alabama

Diane Hogan and her husband, Jim, prepare breakfast for 15 to 20 family members and friends every Christmas Eve morning. They set up a buffet of eggs, cheese grits, sweet rolls, juice, hot tea, coffee, and their favorite—Biscuits and Sausage Gravy.

Tiny Cinnamon Rolls

Transform canned crescent roll dough into these dainty, sweet spirals.

1 (8-ounce) can refrigerated crescent
   rolls
1 tablespoon sugar
1 teaspoon ground cinnamon

⅔ cup sifted powdered sugar
2 teaspoons milk
2 drops of vanilla extract

✦ **Unroll** dough, and separate into 4 rectangles; pinch perforations within rectangles to seal. Stir together 1 tablespoon sugar and cinnamon; sprinkle mixture evenly over rectangles.

✦ **Roll** up, jellyroll fashion, starting with a long side; pinch edges to seal. Gently cut each log into 5 slices, and place, cut side down, in a lightly greased 8- or 9-inch round cakepan.

✦ **Bake** at 375° for 15 minutes or until rolls begin to brown.

✦ **Combine** powdered sugar, milk, and vanilla, stirring until smooth; drizzle over warm rolls. **Yield:** 20 rolls.

Belinda Nix
Rock Hill, South Carolina

Christmas Morning Sticky Buns

½ cup chopped pecans or walnuts
1 (25-ounce) package frozen roll
    dough, thawed
1 (3.4-ounce) package butterscotch
    instant pudding mix

½ cup butter or margarine, melted
½ cup firmly packed brown sugar
¾ teaspoon ground cinnamon

◆ **Sprinkle** pecans in bottom of a buttered 12-cup Bundt pan.

◆ **Arrange** dough in pan; sprinkle with dry pudding mix.

◆ **Stir** together butter, brown sugar, and cinnamon; pour over rolls (mixture will not cover all of dry mix). Cover and chill 8 hours.

◆ **Bake,** uncovered, at 350° for 30 minutes or until golden. Invert onto a serving plate; serve immediately. **Yield:** 8 servings.

Gail H. Reeder
Nashville, Tennessee

This easy recipe is one of Gail Reeder's favorites from her husband's family. She prepares and chills the sweet buns the night before Christmas; then all she has to do in the morning is pop them in the oven.

Praline French Toast

8 large eggs, lightly beaten
1½ cups half-and-half
1 tablespoon brown sugar
2 teaspoons vanilla extract
8 (1-inch-thick) slices French bread

½ cup butter
¾ cup firmly packed brown sugar
½ cup maple syrup
1 (2-ounce) package chopped
    pecans (¾ cup)

◆ **Whisk** together first 4 ingredients in a large bowl until blended. Pour 1 cup egg mixture into a greased 13- x 9-inch baking dish. Place bread in dish; pour remaining egg mixture over bread. Cover and chill 8 hours.

◆ **Stir** together butter and remaining 3 ingredients in a microwave-safe bowl. Cover with heavy-duty plastic wrap, and microwave at HIGH 30 seconds. Pour over bread.

◆ **Bake,** uncovered, at 350° for 30 minutes or until set and golden. **Yield:** 8 servings.

Christmas Breads

Add old-fashioned appeal to casual and elegant holiday meals alike with homemade bread. ✦ Fill your kitchen with the inviting aroma of Onion-Poppy Seed Twist (page 43) baking in the oven. This savory loaf is a favorite at Malinda McDaniel's home, where she offers weary shoppers sustenance with a slice of the warm bread and a bowl of hearty soup. ✦ Easy Stollen (page 41) and Herb Focaccia (page 42) let you make homemade yeast bread fast. The shortcut? Both start with commercial bread dough. ✦ And delicious quick breads, such as Three-Step Biscuits (page 39), also save you time while providing fabulous flavor.

Apricot-Pecan Bread, page 36

Apricot-Pecan Bread

(pictured on page 34)

*This scrumptious quick bread recipe makes two loaves. Give one
to a friend during the holidays, and save the other for your family to enjoy.
It's so moist and delicious, you'd never guess that it's low in fat.*

2½ cups dried apricots, chopped
1 cup chopped pecans
4 cups all-purpose flour, divided
¼ cup butter or margarine, softened
2 cups sugar

2 large eggs
4 teaspoons baking powder
½ teaspoon baking soda
½ teaspoon salt
1½ cups orange juice

✦ **Combine** apricot and warm water to cover in a large bowl; let stand 30
minutes. Drain apricot. Stir in pecans and ½ cup flour; set aside.
✦ **Beat** butter at medium speed with an electric mixer 2 minutes; gradually
add sugar, beating well. Add eggs, one at a time, beating after each addition.
✦ **Combine** remaining 3½ cups flour, baking powder, soda, and salt. Add to
butter mixture alternately with orange juice, beginning and ending with flour
mixture. Stir in apricot mixture.
✦ **Spoon** batter into 2 greased and floured 8- x 4-inch loafpans; let stand at
room temperature 20 minutes.
✦ **Bake** at 350° for 1 hour or until a wooden pick inserted in center comes
out clean. Cool in pans on a wire rack 10 to 15 minutes; remove from pans,
and cool completely on wire rack. **Yield:** 2 loaves.

Marion Sullivan
Charleston, South Carolina

Cumin Bread

3 cups all-purpose flour
2 tablespoons baking powder
½ teaspoon salt
¼ cup sugar
1 tablespoon ground cumin

½ teaspoon dry mustard
2 large eggs, lightly beaten
1⅓ cups milk
⅓ cup vegetable oil
¼ cup picante sauce or salsa

✦ **Stir** together first 6 ingredients in a large bowl; make a well in center of
mixture. Stir together eggs and remaining 3 ingredients; add to dry ingredients,
stirring just until dry ingredients are moistened. Spoon batter into a greased
and floured 9- x 5-inch loafpan.
✦ **Bake** at 350° for 40 minutes or until a toothpick inserted in center comes
out clean. Remove from pan, and cool on a wire rack. **Yield:** 1 loaf.

Corn Spoonbread

1 (8½-ounce) package corn muffin
    mix (we tested with Jiffy)
1 (8-ounce) can cream-style corn
1 (8-ounce) can whole kernel corn,
    drained

1 (8-ounce) container sour cream
½ cup butter or margarine, melted
2 large eggs, lightly beaten

✦ **Stir** together all ingredients in a bowl; pour mixture into a greased 11- x 7-inch baking dish.
✦ **Bake** at 350° for 35 to 40 minutes or until golden. **Yield:** 12 servings.

Alyce S. Emerson
Lexington, Kentucky

This spoonbread from Alyce Emerson is about as easy as it gets! Open a package of muffin mix and a few other convenience items, stir in butter and eggs, and bake.

German Potato Pancakes

(pictured on page 154)

2 large eggs
1 small onion, chopped
1 teaspoon baking powder
¾ teaspoon salt
¼ teaspoon pepper

1½ pounds russet potatoes, peeled
    and cubed
¼ cup all-purpose flour
Sour cream

✦ **Process** first 5 ingredients in a blender until smooth, stopping to scrape down sides. Gradually add potato and flour to blender, processing until mixture is thickened.
✦ **Pour** ¼ cup batter for each pancake into a hot, lightly greased nonstick skillet; cook over medium-high heat 1½ minutes on each side or until browned. Dollop with sour cream. **Yield:** 12 (3-inch) pancakes.

Kathy Wiggins
Nashville, Michigan

Snappy Cheese Biscuits

1½ cups all-purpose flour
1 tablespoon baking powder
½ teaspoon salt
1 tablespoon sugar
⅛ teaspoon ground red pepper

1 cup (4 ounces) shredded sharp
   Cheddar cheese
⅓ cup shortening
½ cup milk

✦ **Stir** together first 5 ingredients in a bowl; cut in cheese and shortening
with a pastry blender until mixture is crumbly. Add milk, stirring just until dry
ingredients are moistened.

✦ **Turn** dough out onto a lightly floured surface; shape into a ball. Pat to
½-inch thickness; cut with a 2-inch round cutter. Place biscuits on an
ungreased baking sheet.

✦ **Bake** at 425° for 10 minutes or until golden. **Yield:** 15 biscuits.

Three-Step Biscuits

*This simple, three-ingredient recipe is worth committing to memory
so that you can have tender homemade biscuits often.*

2 cups self-rising flour

1 (8-ounce) container sour cream

3 tablespoons water

+ **Stir** together all ingredients. (Dough will be crumbly.) Turn dough out onto
a lightly floured surface; knead 3 or 4 times.

+ **Pat** or roll dough to ½-inch thickness; cut with a 2½-inch round cutter.
Place biscuits on a lightly greased baking sheet.

+ **Bake** at 425° for 18 to 20 minutes or until golden. **Yield:** 8 biscuits.

*Mary Sue Spence Cawthon
DeFuniak Springs, Florida*

Fiesta Corn Muffins

2 (6-ounce) packages Mexican
    cornbread mix

2 small red bell peppers, chopped
    (about ½ cup)

2 large eggs, lightly beaten

1 (4.5-ounce) can chopped green
    chiles, undrained

½ cup milk

2 tablespoons vegetable oil

+ **Stir** together cornbread mix and bell pepper in a large bowl; make a well in
center of mixture.

+ **Stir** together eggs and remaining 3 ingredients; add to dry ingredients, stirring just until dry ingredients are moistened.

+ **Spoon** batter into greased muffin pans, filling two-thirds full.

+ **Bake** at 400° for 20 minutes or until golden. Remove muffins from pans
immediately. **Yield:** 1½ dozen.

Fiesta Cornbread: Spread batter into a greased 9-inch square pan. Bake at
400° for 22 minutes or until golden. **Yield:** 9 servings.

Fiesta Corn Sticks: Place well-greased, cast-iron corn stick pans in oven for
3 minutes or until hot. Remove pans from oven; spread batter into pans, filling
three-fourths full. Bake at 400° for 12 minutes or until lightly browned. **Yield:**
1½ dozen.

Blueberry Streusel Muffins

Coating fruit and nuts lightly with flour before stirring them into muffin or cake batter keeps them from sinking to the bottom.

2 cups self-rising flour	1 cup fresh or frozen blueberries
1/3 cup sugar	1/4 cup firmly packed brown sugar
1 large egg, lightly beaten	2 tablespoons self-rising flour
3/4 cup milk	1 tablespoon butter
1/4 cup vegetable oil	1/4 cup chopped almonds (optional)

✦ **Stir** together 2 cups flour and 1/3 cup sugar in a large bowl; set aside 2 tablespoons flour mixture. Make a well in center of remaining mixture.

✦ **Stir** together egg, milk, and oil; add to dry ingredients in bowl, stirring just until dry ingredients are moistened. Gently toss together blueberries and reserved 2 tablespoons flour mixture. Fold blueberries into batter; spoon into greased muffin pans, filling three-fourths full.

✦ **Stir** together brown sugar and 2 tablespoons flour; cut in butter with a pastry cutter until mixture is crumbly. Stir in chopped almonds, if desired. Sprinkle over batter.

✦ **Bake** at 400° for 18 minutes or until lightly browned. Remove from pans immediately. **Yield:** 1 dozen.

Pecan-Orange Muffins

1/2 cup butter or margarine, softened	1 (8-ounce) container plain yogurt
1 cup sugar	3/4 cup chopped pecans, toasted
2 large eggs	1 teaspoon grated orange rind
2 cups all-purpose flour	1/4 cup orange juice
1 teaspoon baking soda	1 tablespoon sugar

✦ **Beat** butter at medium speed with an electric mixer until creamy; gradually add 1 cup sugar, beating well. Add eggs, one at a time, beating until blended after each addition.

✦ **Combine** flour and soda; add to butter mixture alternately with yogurt, beginning and ending with flour mixture. Beat at low speed until blended after each addition. Stir in pecans and orange rind.

✦ **Place** paper baking cups in muffin pans, and lightly coat with vegetable cooking spray. Spoon batter into cups, filling almost full.

✦ **Bake** at 375° for 18 to 20 minutes or until lightly browned. Brush orange juice over hot muffins, and sprinkle evenly with 1 tablespoon sugar. **Yield:** 1 dozen.

Cat Christianson
Brevard, North Carolina

Dana and Cathy "Cat" Christianson enjoy entertaining at their home in the mountains of North Carolina. Over the years Cat has compiled never-fail recipes that keep guests coming back—like these Pecan-Orange Muffins. They are perfect for a holiday brunch.

Easy Stollen

Frozen bread dough speeds up the preparation of this classic German Christmas bread laden with fruit and nuts. The dough will be very elastic, so make sure to press the fruit mixture into the dough until it's incorporated.

½ cup raisins
½ cup chopped walnuts
¼ cup chopped red and green candied cherries
1½ teaspoons orange juice

½ (32-ounce) package frozen bread dough loaves, thawed
1 tablespoon butter, melted
1½ cups sifted powdered sugar
2 to 3 tablespoons orange juice

✦ **Combine** first 4 ingredients. Place dough on a lightly floured surface; press to 1-inch thickness. Spoon fruit mixture onto center of dough; press into dough until evenly distributed. Press dough into a ½-inch-thick oval. Fold in half lengthwise. Pinch seams together.

✦ **Place** on a well-greased baking sheet; brush with butter. Cover and let rise in a warm place (85°), free from drafts, 40 minutes or until doubled in bulk.

✦ **Bake** at 350° for 25 to 30 minutes or until loaf sounds hollow when tapped. Cool on a wire rack 10 minutes.

✦ **Stir** together sugar and orange juice; drizzle over stollen. **Yield:** 1 loaf.

Herb Focaccia

This crispy, crunchy focaccia starts with refrigerated
French bread dough and spends only 10 minutes in the oven.

1 (11-ounce) can refrigerated French bread dough	1 teaspoon freshly ground pepper
2 tablespoons olive oil	1 teaspoon dried oregano
1 teaspoon kosher salt	1 teaspoon dried basil
	½ teaspoon dried thyme

✦ **Unroll** dough into a 15- x 10-inch jellyroll pan; flatten slightly.

✦ **Press** handle of a wooden spoon into dough to make indentations at 1-inch intervals; drizzle dough with oil. Sprinkle with salt and remaining ingredients.

✦ **Bake** at 375° for 10 minutes or until lightly browned. Cut into rectangles; serve warm with marinara sauce, if desired. **Yield:** 8 servings.

Patty Hosch
Marietta, Georgia

Mom's French Bread

North Carolina native Mary Frances Byrne celebrates the holidays each year with recipes that pay homage to the Oregon woods she now calls home. Rustic food—including her mother's warm French bread—graces her table, and Mary Frances serves it all with a generous portion of Southern hospitality.

1 (¼-ounce) envelope active dry yeast	1 teaspoon salt
2 cups warm water (105° to 115°)	¼ cup cornmeal
4½ to 5 cups bread flour, divided	1 egg white, lightly beaten
2 tablespoons sugar	2 tablespoons water
2 tablespoons vegetable oil	

✦ **Combine** yeast and ¼ cup warm water in a 2-cup liquid measuring cup; stir in remaining 1¾ cups warm water, and let stand 5 minutes.

✦ **Stir** together 4 cups flour and sugar in a large bowl. Stir in yeast mixture and oil.

✦ **Cover** and let rise in a warm place (85°), free from drafts, 30 minutes.

✦ **Add** salt and enough remaining ½ to 1 cup flour to make a stiff dough, beating at medium speed with a heavy-duty electric mixer 6 to 8 minutes. Cover and let rise in a warm place, free from drafts, 1 hour or until doubled in bulk.

✦ **Divide** dough in half; shape each portion into a 12-inch loaf.

✦ **Place** each loaf on a lightly greased baking sheet sprinkled with 2 tablespoons cornmeal. Cover and let rise in a warm place, free from drafts, 30 minutes or until doubled in bulk.

✦ **Bake** at 425° for 15 minutes. Stir together egg white and 2 tablespoons water. Brush over loaves, and bake 5 to 10 more minutes or until loaves sound hollow when tapped. **Yield:** 2 loaves.

Mary Frances Byrne
Portland, Oregon

Onion-Poppy Seed Twist

*Slender onion-filled strips of dough are intertwined to create this savory loaf.
Pair it with your favorite soup for a simple, satisfying cold-weather supper.*

2½ cups all-purpose flour, divided
3 tablespoons sugar
1 (¼-ounce) envelope active dry yeast
1 teaspoon salt
½ cup milk
¼ cup water
3 tablespoons butter or margarine
1 large egg, lightly beaten

1 cup diced onion
2 tablespoons poppy seeds
2 tablespoons butter or margarine, melted
⅛ teaspoon salt
1 large egg, lightly beaten
1 tablespoon water
Poppy seeds

✦ **Stir** together 1 cup flour and next 3 ingredients in a large bowl.
✦ **Heat** milk, ¼ cup water, and 3 tablespoons butter in a saucepan until very warm (120° to 130°); gradually stir into flour mixture. Stir in 1 egg and remaining 1½ cups flour until blended.
✦ **Turn** dough out onto a floured surface; knead until smooth and elastic (4 to 6 minutes). Place in a well-greased bowl, turning to grease top. Cover and let stand 10 minutes.
✦ **Stir** together onion and next 3 ingredients in a small bowl.
✦ **Roll** dough into a 14- x 10-inch rectangle; cut in half lengthwise. Spoon half of onion mixture down center of each rectangle. Bring long sides over filling, pinching seams to seal.
✦ **Place,** seam side down and side by side, on a lightly greased baking sheet. Pinch portions together at 1 end to seal; twist portions, and pinch ends to seal. Cover and let rise in a warm place (85°), free from drafts, 20 to 30 minutes or until doubled in bulk.
✦ **Stir** together 1 egg and 1 tablespoon water; brush over dough. Sprinkle dough with poppy seeds.
✦ **Bake** at 350° for 35 minutes, shielding with aluminum foil after 25 minutes; cool on a wire rack. **Yield:** 1 loaf.

*Malinda McDaniel
Memphis, Tennessee*

Malinda McDaniel's house just may be the most relaxing place in Memphis on a Saturday before Christmas. At her "Soup Kitchen for Weary (or Not So Weary) Shoppers," friends can sit down for soup and bread served by Malinda, Judy Rutherford, and Robbie Lowery.

"I have a small house," says Malinda, "and this revolving approach allows us to entertain everyone we want to invite."

Serve a slice of Onion-Poppy Seed Twist with homemade soup for a soothing after-shopping meal.

Refrigerator Yeast Rolls

1 cup shortening
1 cup sugar
2 teaspoons salt
1 cup boiling water
2 large eggs, lightly beaten
2 (¼-ounce) envelopes active dry yeast

1 cup warm water (105° to 115°)
6 cups all-purpose flour
¼ cup butter or margarine, melted

✦ **Stir** together first 3 ingredients in a large bowl; stir in 1 cup boiling water. Cool. Stir in eggs.

✦ **Combine** yeast and warm water in a 1-cup liquid measuring cup; let stand 5 minutes. Stir into egg mixture. Gradually add flour, stirring until blended. Cover and chill at least 4 hours.

✦ **Pinch** off one-third of dough. Cover and chill remaining dough up to 5 days, if desired.

✦ **Roll** dough to ¼-inch thickness on a floured surface. Cut with a 2-inch round cutter.

♦ **Place** 2 inches apart on lightly greased baking sheets. Brush with melted butter. Let rise at room temperature 1 hour or until doubled in bulk.
♦ **Bake** at 375° for 10 to 12 minutes or until rolls are golden. **Yield:** about 1½ dozen per portion.

Hazel L. McCurry
West Union, South Carolina

Cinnamon Rolls: Roll one-third of dough into a 14- x 10-inch rectangle. Brush with ¼ cup melted butter; sprinkle with ⅓ cup sugar and 2 teaspoons ground cinnamon. Roll up, starting at long end; cut crosswise into ¾-inch-thick slices. Place in 2 lightly greased 9-inch round cakepans. Let rise and bake as directed. Stir together ½ cup powdered sugar and 2 teaspoons milk; drizzle glaze over warm rolls. **Yield:** about 1½ dozen per portion.

Herb Rolls: Follow procedure for Cinnamon Rolls, substituting 1 tablespoon each of chopped fresh chives, basil, and rosemary for sugar and cinnamon. Let rise and bake as directed. Omit glaze. **Yield:** about 1½ dozen per portion.

Sweet Potato Rolls

1 quart water	6¼ cups all purpose flour, divided
1 (¾-pound) sweet potato, peeled and chopped	1½ teaspoons salt
3 tablespoons sugar, divided	1 cup milk
1 (¼-ounce) envelope active dry yeast	1 tablespoon vegetable oil
	2 large eggs, lightly beaten

♦ **Bring** water to a boil; add potato. Cook 10 to 15 minutes or until tender. Drain, reserving 1 cup liquid; cool liquid to 110°. Mash potato; stir in 2 tablespoons sugar. Set aside. Stir remaining 1 tablespoon sugar and yeast into reserved liquid; let stand 10 minutes.
♦ **Stir** together 5½ cups flour and salt in a large bowl; make a well in center of mixture. Stir together potato mixture, milk, oil, and eggs; add yeast mixture, stirring until blended. Add to flour mixture, stirring to make a soft dough.
♦ **Turn** dough out onto a floured surface; knead lightly, adding ½ cup flour, as needed, to prevent sticking. Place dough in a well-greased bowl, turning to grease top. Cover and let rise in a warm place (85°), free from drafts, 1 hour or until doubled in bulk. Punch dough down; turn out onto floured surface, and divide in half. Shape each portion into an 18- x 2½-inch log.
♦ **Cut** each log diagonally into 1-inch-thick slices; sprinkle slices with remaining ¼ cup flour. Place 1 to 2 inches apart on lightly greased baking sheets.
♦ **Cover** and let rise in a warm place, free from drafts, 20 minutes. Bake at 400° for 15 to 20 minutes or until golden. Cool on wire racks. **Yield:** 2½ dozen.

Cat Christianson
Brevard, North Carolina

Spoon Rolls

Mouthwatering homemade rolls have never been so simple; just spoon the dough into muffin cups. The rolls don't even need to rise. They bake up warm and yeasty, with slightly pebbly tops that resemble muffins.

1 (¼-ounce) envelope active dry yeast
2 tablespoons warm water (105° to 115°)
½ cup vegetable oil
¼ cup sugar
4 cups self-rising flour
2 cups warm milk or water (105° to 115°)
1 large egg, lightly beaten

✦ **Combine** yeast and 2 tablespoons warm water in a 1-cup liquid measuring cup; let stand 5 minutes.

✦ **Stir** together yeast mixture, oil, and remaining ingredients in a large bowl; stir until smooth. Cover tightly, and chill at least 4 hours or up to 4 days.

✦ **Stir** batter. Spoon into greased muffin pans, filling three-fourths full. Bake at 350° for 25 minutes or until golden. **Yield:** 20 rolls.

Janet Williams
Franklin, Tennessee

Make-Ahead Crescent Rolls

(pictured on page 152)

*These rolls are ideal for Christmas dinner because you can make
and freeze them up to a month before serving.*

1 (1/4-ounce) envelope active dry yeast	1 1/2 teaspoons salt
1/4 cup warm water (105° to 115°)	3 1/2 cups all-purpose flour, divided
1 cup milk	1 large egg, lightly beaten
1/2 cup shortening	2 tablespoons butter or margarine,
1/4 cup sugar	melted

✦ **Combine** yeast and warm water in a 1-cup liquid measuring cup; let stand
5 minutes.

✦ **Stir** together milk and next 3 ingredients in a heavy saucepan; heat until
shortening melts, stirring occasionally. Cool to 105° to 115°.

✦ **Stir** together yeast mixture and milk mixture in a large mixing bowl; add
1 1/2 cups flour, and beat at medium speed with an electric mixer until blended.
Stir in egg until blended.

✦ **Beat** in enough of remaining 2 cups flour to make a soft dough. Place in a
well-greased bowl, turning to grease top.

✦ **Cover** and let rise in a warm place (85°), free from drafts, 1 1/2 hours or until
doubled in bulk.

✦ **Punch** dough down, and divide into thirds; roll each portion into a 9-inch
circle on a lightly floured surface. Brush with butter, and cut each portion into
8 wedges. Roll up each wedge tightly, beginning at wide end. Place, point side
down, on a greased baking sheet, and bend into crescent shapes.

✦ **Cover** and let rise in a warm place, free from drafts, 45 minutes or until
doubled in bulk.

✦ **Bake** at 400° for 8 minutes or just until lightly browned; cool on baking
sheets on wire racks. Cover and freeze until firm. Place frozen rolls in heavy-
duty, zip-top plastic freezer bags; seal and freeze up to 1 month.

✦ **Remove** crescent rolls from freezer; place on baking sheets, and thaw at
room temperature.

✦ **Bake** at 400° for 5 to 7 minutes or until lightly browned. **Yield:** 2 dozen.

Louise McGehee
Montevallo, Alabama

Cozy Casual Entrées

*S*low down during the hectic holidays and enjoy the company of friends and family over an easygoing meal. ✦ Take a break from elaborate dinners with Mary Kiley McMenamin's down-home Southern supper of Timely Fried Chicken (page 58), corn pudding, cheese grits, green beans, and hush puppies. ✦ Invite carolers in from the cold with a bowl of warming White Christmas Chili (page 59) or 1-2-3 Jambalaya (page 53). ✦ Prepare and freeze Make-Ahead Company Beef Stew (page 60) in late November, and in December you'll have a hearty meal on hand. ✦ These comforting main dishes offer casual entertaining options for almost any occasion.

Spicy Pasta and Shrimp, page 56

Marinated Roast Beef

1 cup vegetable oil
¾ cup soy sauce
½ cup lemon juice
¼ cup Worcestershire sauce

¼ cup prepared mustard
30 garlic cloves, cut in half
1 (6- to 8-pound) beef rump roast
1 tablespoon freshly ground pepper

✦ **Combine** first 6 ingredients in a large heavy-duty, zip-top plastic bag. Pierce roast at 1-inch intervals with a meat fork; place roast in bag. Seal bag; chill 24 to 48 hours, turning roast occasionally.

✦ **Remove** roast from marinade, discarding marinade. Place roast on a lightly greased rack in a broiler pan; sprinkle with pepper.

✦ **Bake** at 325° for 1 hour and 50 minutes or until a meat thermometer registers 145° (medium-rare) to 160° (medium). Let stand 10 minutes before slicing. **Yield:** 10 to 12 servings.

Catherine Rowsey
Bartlett, Tennessee

Sauerbraten

(pictured on page 154)

Virginia native Kathy Wiggins and her husband, Don, celebrate the holidays with age-old German traditions handed down from her parents. They serve Sauerbraten as part of their authentic German menu (see menu, page 154). Kathy and her mother share the preparations, making the holiday more meaningful—and manageable.

3 tablespoons pickling spice
1 cup dry red wine
1 cup red wine vinegar
1 cup water
1 tablespoon salt
½ teaspoon pepper
2 bay leaves
2 onions, sliced

1 carrot, sliced
1 (4-pound) sirloin tip roast
3 tablespoons vegetable oil
¼ cup all-purpose flour
1 tablespoon sugar
¾ cup crushed gingersnaps
 (about 12 cookies)

✦ **Tie** pickling spice in a cheesecloth bag. Combine bag, wine, and next 7 ingredients in a shallow dish; add roast. Cover; chill 8 hours, turning occasionally.

✦ **Remove** roast from marinade, reserving marinade. Brown roast on all sides in hot oil in a Dutch oven. Remove roast, reserving drippings. Whisk flour and sugar into drippings; cook over medium-high heat, whisking constantly, 2 minutes or until browned. Gradually stir in reserved marinade.

✦ **Return** roast to Dutch oven; bring mixture to a boil. Cover, reduce heat, and simmer 2½ hours. Discard spice bag and bay leaves. Remove roast, reserving drippings in pan; slice roast, and keep warm.

✦ **Stir** gingersnaps into reserved drippings; simmer, stirring constantly, 2 minutes. Pour mixture through a colander into a bowl. Press vegetables through colander with back of a spoon. Serve gravy with roast. **Yield:** 8 servings.

Kathy Wiggins
Nashville, Michigan

All-in-One Spaghetti

A slow cooker makes this spaghetti a snap to prepare and cuts cleanup time.

1 pound ground beef
2 garlic cloves, minced
1 large onion, chopped
3 cups tomato juice
1 cup water
1 teaspoon salt
1 teaspoon sugar
2 to 3 teaspoons chili powder

1 teaspoon dried oregano
Dash of pepper
1 (8-ounce) can tomato sauce
1 (6-ounce) can tomato paste
1 (7-ounce) package dried spaghetti, uncooked
Grated Parmesan cheese (optional)
Garnish: fresh Italian parsley sprigs

✦ **Cook** first 3 ingredients in a Dutch oven, stirring until beef crumbles and is no longer pink; drain well. Return to Dutch oven.

✦ **Stir** in tomato juice and next 8 ingredients; bring to a boil. Cover, reduce heat, and simmer, stirring often, 30 minutes.

✦ **Add** pasta; cover and simmer, stirring often, 20 minutes or until pasta is tender. If desired, sprinkle each serving with Parmesan cheese, and garnish.
Yield: 6 servings.

Nancy K. Ayers
Blacksburg, Virginia

Thai Lemon Beef

1 (1-inch-thick) boneless top round
   steak
⅓ cup soy sauce
¼ cup lemon juice
¼ cup water
1 tablespoon dried crushed red pepper

4 garlic cloves, minced
1 tablespoon vegetable oil
4 green onions, cut into 2-inch pieces
2 carrots, thinly sliced
2 teaspoons cornstarch
Hot cooked ramen noodles or rice

✦ **Cut** steak diagonally across grain into ⅛-inch-thick strips, and place in a medium bowl.
✦ **Stir** together soy sauce and next 4 ingredients. Reserve half of mixture. Pour remaining mixture over steak. Cover and chill 30 minutes. Drain steak, discarding marinade.
✦ **Stir-fry** half of steak in ½ tablespoon hot oil in a large nonstick skillet over medium-high heat 1 minute or until beef is no longer pink. Remove from skillet; repeat procedure with remaining steak and oil. Remove beef from skillet.
✦ **Add** onions and carrot to skillet; stir-fry 3 minutes or until crisp-tender.
✦ **Whisk** cornstarch into reserved soy sauce mixture; stir into vegetables, and stir-fry until thickened. Add steak; stir-fry until thoroughly heated. Serve over noodles. **Yield:** 4 servings.

Pork Chops with Black-and-White Salsa

1 (16-ounce) can black beans, drained
1 (16-ounce) can great Northern
   beans, drained
1 (14½-ounce) can Mexican-style
   tomatoes, drained and chopped
¼ cup chopped purple onion
2 small jalapeño peppers, chopped
2 garlic cloves, minced

¼ cup chopped fresh cilantro
3 tablespoons white wine vinegar
½ teaspoon sugar
½ teaspoon salt
⅛ teaspoon pepper
4 (1½-inch-thick) boneless pork loin
   chops
Garnish: fresh cilantro sprigs

✦ **Combine** first 11 ingredients, stirring gently. Cover salsa; chill at least 1 hour.
✦ **Grill** pork chops, covered with grill lid, over medium heat (300° to 350°)
5 minutes on each side or to desired degree of doneness. Serve chops immediately with salsa. Garnish, if desired. **Yield:** 4 servings.

Molasses-Grilled Pork Tenderloin

¼ cup molasses
2 tablespoons coarse-grained Dijon
   mustard

1 tablespoon apple cider vinegar
4 (¾-pound) pork tenderloins, trimmed

✦ **Stir** together first 3 ingredients; brush over tenderloins. Cover and marinate in refrigerator 8 hours.
✦ **Grill,** covered with grill lid, over medium-high heat (350° to 400°) about 10 minutes on each side or until a meat thermometer inserted in thickest portion registers 160°. **Yield:** 8 servings.

Grilled Ham and Apples

½ cup orange marmalade
2 teaspoons butter or margarine
¼ teaspoon ground ginger

2 (½-inch-thick) ham slices (about
   2½ pounds)
4 apples, cut into ½-inch-thick slices

✦ **Stir** together first 3 ingredients in a 1-cup liquid measuring cup; microwave at HIGH 1 minute or until melted, stirring once.
✦ **Grill** ham and apple, covered with grill lid, over medium-high heat (350° to 400°), turning occasionally and basting with marmalade mixture, 20 minutes or until thoroughly heated. **Yield:** 4 servings.

1-2-3 Jambalaya

This easy one-dish meal is hearty enough to warm you during winter's chill.

1 large onion, diced
1 large green bell pepper, diced
1 pound smoked sausage, cut into
   ¼-inch slices
1 tablespoon olive oil
4 cups chopped cooked chicken
3 cups uncooked long-grain rice

2 (10½-ounce) cans French onion
   soup, undiluted
1 (14½-ounce) can chicken broth
1 (14½-ounce) can beef broth
2 to 3 teaspoons Creole seasoning
2 to 3 teaspoons hot sauce
Garnish: fresh cilantro sprigs

✦ **Sauté** first 3 ingredients in hot oil in an ovenproof Dutch oven 4 to 5 minutes or until sausage browns.
✦ **Stir** in chicken and next 6 ingredients.
✦ **Bake,** covered, at 350° for 40 minutes, stirring after 30 minutes. Garnish, if desired. **Yield:** 8 to 10 servings.

Darryl R. Turgeon
New Orleans, Louisiana

New Orleans Red Beans and Rice

1 pound dried red beans
7 cups water
1 green bell pepper, chopped
1 medium onion, chopped
3 celery ribs, chopped

3 garlic cloves, chopped
½ pound andouille sausage, sliced
3 tablespoons Creole seasoning
Hot cooked rice
Garnish: sliced green onions

✦ **Layer** first 8 ingredients in a 4-quart slow cooker.
✦ **Cook,** covered, at HIGH 7 hours or until beans are tender. Serve with hot cooked rice. Garnish, if desired. **Yield:** 3½ quarts.

Janet Rush-Pugh
Biloxi, Mississippi

Pasta with Broccoli and Sausage

(pictured on facing page)

Serve crisp greens alongside this hearty sausage dish for a quick, casual holiday dinner.

1 pound fresh broccoli, cut into
  flowerets
1 (9-ounce) package refrigerated
  fettuccine
2 tablespoons butter or margarine
1 cup sliced fresh mushrooms
1 garlic clove, minced

1 pound reduced-fat smoked sausage,
  sliced
3 large eggs
¾ cup whipping cream
¾ teaspoon pepper
1 cup grated Parmesan cheese

✦ **Cook** broccoli and fettuccine in boiling water to cover in a Dutch oven 4 minutes or until broccoli is crisp-tender; drain. Rinse with cold water; drain. Place in a large bowl.
✦ **Melt** butter in a large heavy skillet; add mushrooms and garlic, and sauté 3 minutes or until tender. Add to pasta mixture.
✦ **Brown** sausage in skillet over medium-high heat, stirring occasionally, 5 minutes; drain. Add to pasta mixture. Wipe skillet clean with a paper towel.
✦ **Stir** together eggs, whipping cream, and pepper in skillet until blended. Add pasta mixture; toss well.
✦ **Cook** over low heat, stirring constantly, 3 to 5 minutes or until mixture is thickened. Sprinkle with Parmesan cheese, and toss. Serve immediately. **Yield:** 4 servings.

Beth Poland
Louisville, Kentucky

Pasta with
Broccoli and Sausage

Snapper with Rosemary Sauce

½ cup all-purpose flour
½ teaspoon salt
¼ teaspoon pepper
1¼ pounds snapper fillets

¼ cup olive oil
¼ cup white wine vinegar
½ teaspoon chopped fresh rosemary
2 garlic cloves, pressed

✦ **Stir** together first 3 ingredients. Dredge fish in mixture.
✦ **Heat** oil in a large skillet over medium-high heat until hot; add fish, and cook 3 to 4 minutes on each side or until golden. Transfer fish to a serving platter, and keep warm.
✦ **Add** vinegar, rosemary, and garlic to skillet; cook over high heat 1 minute, stirring constantly to loosen particles from bottom. Pour sauce over fish, and serve immediately. **Yield:** 4 servings.

Mary Pappas
Richmond, Virginia

Spicy Pasta and Shrimp

(pictured on page 48)

8 ounces uncooked dried linguine
½ pound unpeeled medium-size fresh
   shrimp
2 tablespoons butter or margarine
¼ cup chopped green onions
1 or 2 garlic cloves, minced
1 tablespoon Cajun or Creole
   seasoning

½ cup whipping cream
¼ cup dry white wine
⅓ cup freshly grated Parmesan cheese
1 to 2 teaspoons dried crushed red
   pepper
⅓ cup chopped fresh parsley

✦ **Cook** linguine according to package directions; keep warm.
✦ **Peel** shrimp; devein, if desired. Set aside.
✦ **Melt** butter in a large skillet; add green onions and garlic. Sauté until tender. Stir in Cajun seasoning and shrimp; cook, stirring constantly, 1 minute.
✦ **Stir** in whipping cream; reduce heat, and simmer 3 minutes, stirring often. Stir in wine; simmer 3 minutes, stirring occasionally.
✦ **Stir** in linguine, Parmesan cheese, and crushed red pepper; cook, stirring gently, until thoroughly heated. Stir in parsley, and serve immediately. **Yield:** 2 to 3 servings.

Robert D. Betzel
Marietta, Georgia

Chicken Fettuccine Supreme

1 (12-ounce) package dried fettuccine
6 skinned and boned chicken breast
　　halves
¼ teaspoon salt
¼ teaspoon black pepper
¼ cup butter
1 garlic clove, minced
1 large green bell pepper, chopped
1 large red bell pepper, chopped
1 (17-ounce) jar Alfredo sauce
1 cup chopped pecans, toasted
Freshly grated Parmesan cheese

✦ **Cook** pasta according to package directions. Drain; set aside, and keep warm.

✦ **Sprinkle** chicken with salt and ¼ teaspoon pepper. Melt butter in a large skillet; cook chicken in butter 5 minutes on each side or until done. Remove chicken from skillet, reserving drippings in pan. Slice chicken diagonally into strips, and set aside.

✦ **Add** garlic and bell peppers to skillet; cook, stirring constantly, until tender.

✦ **Combine** bell pepper mixture, Alfredo sauce, pecans, and pasta; toss gently. To serve, spoon pasta mixture evenly onto 6 individual serving plates; top evenly with chicken, and sprinkle with Parmesan cheese. Serve immediately. **Yield:** 6 servings.

Chicken and Dumplings

1 (3-pound) whole chicken, cut up
¼ cup chicken bouillon granules
1 teaspoon pepper
2 cups all-purpose flour
1 tablespoon baking powder
1 teaspoon salt
¼ cup shortening
⅔ to ¾ cup milk
4 hard-cooked eggs, chopped

✦ **Bring** chicken and water to cover to a boil in a large Dutch oven; reduce heat, and simmer 1 hour. Remove chicken; cool. Pour broth through a wire-mesh strainer into a large saucepan, discarding solids. Skim off fat. Return broth to Dutch oven; bring to a simmer.

✦ **Skin** and bone chicken. Cut chicken into bite-size pieces; add chicken pieces, bouillon granules, and pepper to broth. Return to a simmer.

✦ **Stir** together flour, baking powder, and salt in a bowl. Cut in shortening with a pastry blender until mixture is crumbly. Add milk, stirring just until dry ingredients are moistened.

✦ **Turn** dough out onto a lightly floured surface. Roll out to ⅛-inch thickness; sprinkle lightly with flour, and cut into 3- x 2-inch strips.

✦ **Bring** broth mixture to a boil. Drop strips, one at a time, into boiling broth, stirring gently, until all are added. Reduce heat, and simmer, stirring often, 20 minutes. Stir in egg just before serving. **Yield:** 6 to 8 servings.

Jenne E. Crutchley
Hoover, Alabama

Timely Fried Chicken

(pictured below and on pages 148 and 153)

*Chilling the chicken after dredging it in a flour mixture helps
give it an extracrispy coating during frying.*

3 cups all-purpose flour
2 teaspoons paprika
1½ teaspoons salt
3 large eggs
⅓ cup milk
2 tablespoons lemon juice
2 (2- to 3-pound) whole chickens,
  cut up
Vegetable oil
Garnish: fresh sage leaves

✦ **Stir** together first 3 ingredients in a shallow dish.

✦ **Whisk** together eggs, milk, and lemon juice in a bowl.

✦ **Dredge** chicken in flour mixture, dip in egg mixture, and dredge again in
flour mixture. Cover and chill 2 hours.

✦ **Pour** oil to depth of ½ inch into an electric skillet; heat to 375°.

✦ **Fry** chicken, in batches, 10 minutes on each side or until golden. Reduce
heat to 250°; cover and cook 25 minutes or until done. Drain on paper towels.
Garnish, if desired. **Yield:** 8 to 10 servings.

Mary Kiley McMenamin
Melrose, Massachusetts

Rosemary-Orange Turkey Breast

1 (1½- to 2-pound) skinned and
    boned turkey breast
½ cup fresh orange juice
3 tablespoons olive oil
2 tablespoons balsamic vinegar

1 tablespoon honey
2 teaspoons dried rosemary, crushed
1 teaspoon salt
⅛ teaspoon dried crushed red pepper
Garnish: orange slices

✦ **Place** turkey breast between 2 sheets of heavy-duty plastic wrap; flatten to
1-inch thickness, using a meat mallet or a rolling pin. Place turkey in a large
heavy-duty, zip-top plastic bag.

✦ **Combine** orange juice and next 6 ingredients in a jar. Cover tightly, and
shake vigorously. Pour marinade over turkey; seal bag. Marinate in refrigerator
8 hours, turning occasionally. Remove turkey from marinade, reserving marinade. Bring marinade to a boil in a small saucepan; remove from heat.

✦ **Grill** turkey, covered with grill lid, over medium-high heat (350° to 400°)
15 minutes or until meat thermometer inserted into the thickest portion registers 170°, turning and basting occasionally with marinade. Cut turkey into
serving-size pieces. Garnish, if desired. **Yield:** 6 servings.

White Christmas Chili

(pictured on page 153)

8 skinned and boned chicken breast
    halves
2 medium onions, chopped
2 garlic cloves, minced
1 tablespoon vegetable oil
2 (14½-ounce) cans chicken broth
4 (15-ounce) cans cannellini beans,
    rinsed and drained
1 (15-ounce) can cannellini beans,
    rinsed, drained, and mashed
2 (4.5-ounce) cans chopped green
    chiles, undrained

1 teaspoon salt
¾ teaspoon dried oregano
1 teaspoon ground cumin
½ teaspoon chili powder
½ teaspoon ground black pepper
⅛ teaspoon ground cloves
⅛ teaspoon ground red pepper
Toppings: sour cream, shredded
    Monterey Jack cheese with
    jalapeño peppers, chopped
    fresh cilantro

✦ **Cut** chicken into bite-size pieces.

✦ **Sauté** chicken, onion, and garlic in hot oil in a Dutch oven over medium-
high heat 10 minutes or until chicken is done.

✦ **Stir** in broth and next 10 ingredients; bring to a boil. Reduce heat, and
simmer, uncovered, 30 minutes. Serve with desired toppings. **Yield:** 10 cups.

Tina Fortier-Bording Vanderwall
Sherrill, New York

> ········ ✦ ········
>
> *"Food experienced in
> the South seems to
> have more than just
> ingredients in it. . . . If
> you can eat catfish
> after having eaten it
> in a ramshackle café
> in Mississippi, or taste
> sweet potato pie as
> a reminder of the
> neighborhood festival
> in St. Augustine,
> Florida, those memo-
> ries add a special
> flavor to any dish."*
>
> *—Tina Fortier-
> Bording Vanderwall*

Make-Ahead Company Beef Stew

(pictured on page 152)

Warmth and hospitality come straight from the freezer with this hearty stew.
Turn to page 152 to find a complete make-ahead menu for the holidays.

1 (3-pound) boneless chuck roast, cut into 1-inch cubes
1 large onion, sliced
1 garlic clove, minced
1 tablespoon dried parsley flakes
½ teaspoon salt
½ teaspoon pepper
½ teaspoon dried thyme
1 bay leaf
1 cup dry red wine
2 tablespoons olive oil

4 bacon slices, cut crosswise into ¼-inch pieces
3 tablespoons all-purpose flour
1½ cups beef broth
½ pound baby carrots
1 (16-ounce) package frozen pearl onions
2 tablespoons butter or margarine
1 (8-ounce) package fresh mushrooms
Mashed Potato Bowls (see facing page)
Garnishes: fresh thyme sprigs, fresh chives

✦ **Combine** first 8 ingredients in a shallow dish or heavy-duty, zip-top plastic bag. Combine wine and oil; pour over meat mixture. Cover or seal; chill 1 hour. Drain well, reserving marinade.

✦ **Cook** bacon in an ovenproof Dutch oven until crisp; remove bacon, reserving drippings in Dutch oven. Drain bacon on paper towels. Place in a heavy-duty, zip-top plastic bag; seal and freeze.

✦ **Brown** beef in reserved bacon drippings. Drain and return to Dutch oven; sprinkle with flour, and cook, stirring constantly, 1 to 2 minutes. Add reserved marinade and broth; bring to a boil.

✦ **Bake,** covered, at 300° for 1 hour and 30 minutes or until tender. Add carrots and pearl onions; bake 30 more minutes.

✦ **Melt** butter in a large skillet. Add mushrooms; sauté until tender. Add to beef mixture. Cool and spoon into a freezer container; cover and freeze up to 1 month.

✦ **Remove** bacon and stew from freezer; thaw in refrigerator overnight. Place stew in a Dutch oven; cook over medium heat, stirring occasionally. Discard bay leaf. Serve in Mashed Potato Bowls. Sprinkle with bacon; garnish, if desired. **Yield:** 6 cups.

Mashed Potato Bowls

4 large potatoes (3 pounds)
2 teaspoons salt, divided
1 (8-ounce) package cream cheese, softened
1 large egg, lightly beaten
2 tablespoons all-purpose flour
¼ teaspoon baking powder
1 tablespoon butter or margarine, melted
¼ teaspoon paprika

✦ **Cook** potatoes, 1 teaspoon salt, and boiling water to cover in a Dutch oven 25 minutes or until tender. Drain and cool to touch.

✦ **Peel** potatoes; mash in a large bowl, using a potato masher. Stir in remaining 1 teaspoon salt, cream cheese, and next 3 ingredients until blended.

✦ **Spoon** mixture into 6 large mounds on a baking sheet. Shape each mound into a 4-inch bowl, using the back of a large serving spoon; cover and freeze until firm. Place frozen bowls in heavy-duty, zip-top plastic bags; freeze up to 1 month.

✦ **Remove** bowls from freezer; place frozen bowls on a lightly greased baking sheet. Brush with butter, and sprinkle with paprika.

✦ **Bake** frozen bowls at 450° for 15 minutes or until thoroughly heated and lightly browned. **Yield:** 6 potato bowls.

Stanlay Webber
Winston-Salem, North Carolina

Easy Potato-Sausage Soup

½ pound ground pork sausage
16 ounces frozen hash brown potatoes (4 cups)
1 large onion, chopped
1 (14½-ounce) can chicken broth
2 cups water
1 (10¾-ounce) can cream of celery soup, undiluted
1 (10¾-ounce) can cream of chicken soup, undiluted
2 cups milk
Garnish: shredded Cheddar cheese

✦ **Brown** sausage in a large Dutch oven over medium heat, stirring until it crumbles and is no longer pink. Drain; return to Dutch oven.

✦ **Add** hash brown potatoes and next 3 ingredients; bring to a boil. Cover, reduce heat, and simmer 30 minutes. Stir in soups and milk; cook, stirring often, until thoroughly heated. Garnish, if desired. **Yield:** 10 cups.

Ham 'n' Pot Liquor Soup

Ham 'n' Pot Liquor Soup

(pictured on facing page)

*Soothe your frazzled holiday nerves with a bowl of
this comforting soup and a wedge of cornbread.*

2 pounds fresh collard greens
1 (2-pound) ham steak, chopped
2 tablespoons hot sauce
3 tablespoons olive oil
3 medium onions, chopped
1 garlic clove, minced
6 red potatoes, diced
3 (14½-ounce) cans chicken broth

2 (16-ounce) cans field peas, drained
2 (16-ounce) cans crowder peas, drained
2 cups water
½ cup vermouth
1 tablespoon white vinegar
1 teaspoon salt

✦ **Remove** and discard stems and discolored spots from collard greens; rinse with cold water. Drain; tear into 1-inch pieces. Bring collard greens and water to cover to a boil in a large Dutch oven. Remove from heat, and drain. Repeat procedure once. Remove collard greens from Dutch oven.

✦ **Toss** together chopped ham and hot sauce; cook in hot oil in Dutch oven over medium-high heat 8 to 10 minutes or until browned. Add onion and garlic; sauté until tender. Stir in collards, potato, and remaining ingredients; bring to a boil. Reduce heat; simmer, stirring occasionally, 45 minutes. **Yield:** 10 cups.

Brooks Hart
Woodbury, Connecticut

When Brooks Hart plans holiday meals, thoughts of the South Carolina Lowcountry are never far away.

"My grandmother, from Clover, South Carolina, cooked very simply without a lot of fat," he says.

Here, he shares one of his signature soups, patterned after his grandmother's style of cooking.

Tempting Turkey Soup

3 cups water
1 (10¾-ounce) can cream of chicken soup, undiluted
1 (14.5-ounce) can stewed tomatoes
2 to 3 cups chopped cooked turkey
5 small potatoes, peeled and cut into ½-inch cubes
3 carrots, scraped and chopped
1 medium onion, chopped

1 garlic clove, minced
2 chicken bouillon cubes
1 teaspoon salt
1 teaspoon dried basil
½ teaspoon dried thyme
¼ teaspoon pepper
½ teaspoon poultry seasoning (optional)
1½ cups milk
2 tablespoons chopped fresh cilantro

✦ **Bring** first 13 ingredients, and, if desired, poultry seasoning, to a boil in a Dutch oven. Reduce heat, and simmer, stirring occasionally, 30 minutes or until vegetables are tender. Stir in milk and cilantro; cook, stirring often, just until thoroughly heated. **Yield:** 10 cups.

Mrs. Wesley Eastridge
Kingsport, Tennessee

Mexican Cheese Soup

½ cup diced green bell pepper
½ cup minced onion
¼ cup butter or margarine, melted
⅓ cup all-purpose flour
2 (10½-ounce) cans condensed chicken broth, undiluted
4 cups (16 ounces) shredded Monterey Jack cheese

½ teaspoon ground cumin
½ teaspoon dried oregano
½ teaspoon ground red pepper
1 (4.5-ounce) can chopped green chiles, undrained
1 cup half-and-half

✦ **Sauté** bell pepper and onion in butter in a large saucepan over medium-high heat 3 to 4 minutes or until tender. Add flour; cook, stirring constantly, 2 minutes. Gradually add broth; cook, stirring constantly, 4 minutes or until thickened. Reduce heat. Stir in cheese and next 4 ingredients.

✦ **Simmer,** stirring often, 10 minutes. Stir in half-and-half; simmer, stirring often, 5 minutes or until thoroughly heated. **Yield:** about 6 cups.

Marsha Thompson
Wilmington, North Carolina

Carrot-Butternut Squash Soup

Growing up in South Carolina, Patricia Agnew ate vegetables cooked in fat and meat at every meal. These days she cooks with a lighter touch. She says, "When I went away to college, I discovered that the fresh flavors of vegetables are wonderful on their own, and meat is not required at every meal."

Now, she has a stockpile of terrific low-fat recipes. Here's one of her best.

2 garlic cloves, minced
1 medium onion, chopped
2 tablespoons olive oil, divided
1 pound carrots, shredded
1 butternut squash, peeled and shredded
2 (14½-ounce) cans low-sodium fat-free chicken broth

½ cup cooked long-grain rice
8 (½-inch-thick) French bread slices
1½ cups fat-free milk
1 tablespoon grated orange rind
½ teaspoon salt
¼ teaspoon pepper
¼ cup chopped fresh parsley

✦ **Sauté** garlic and onion in 1 tablespoon hot oil in a large Dutch oven 2 minutes or until tender. Add carrot and squash; sauté 5 minutes or until tender.

✦ **Add** broth; bring to a boil. Reduce heat, and simmer 20 minutes. Stir in rice. Remove from heat; cool slightly.

✦ **Cut** bread slices into 1-inch triangles; brush with remaining 1 tablespoon oil. Arrange on a baking sheet. Bake at 350° for 10 minutes or until lightly toasted.

✦ **Process** vegetable mixture, in batches, in a blender until smooth, stopping once to scrape down sides; return to Dutch oven. Stir in milk, and simmer until thoroughly heated. Stir in orange rind, salt, and pepper.

✦ **Dip** 1 point of each bread triangle in soup, and coat with parsley. Serve croutons on soup. **Yield:** 8 cups.

Patricia Agnew
Charleston, South Carolina

Oven-Grilled
Reuben, page 67

Easy Vegetable Chowder

Easy Vegetable Chowder

*A bowl of this steaming chowder and a thick, crisp Oven-Grilled
Reuben (page 67) create cozy simplicity.*

11 new potatoes
2 large carrots
1 large onion
3 tablespoons olive oil
2 (10¾-ounce) cans Cheddar cheese
    soup, undiluted
4 cups water

1 (1-ounce) envelope dry onion
    soup mix
1 teaspoon pepper
½ cup sliced green onions
Garnishes: sliced green onions,
    shredded Cheddar cheese

✦ **Cut** potatoes into ½-inch cubes and carrots into ½-inch slices; coarsely chop
onion.

✦ **Sauté** potato, carrot, and chopped onion in hot oil in a Dutch oven until
vegetables are tender.

✦ **Stir** together Cheddar cheese soup and next 3 ingredients; add to vegetable
mixture. Bring to a boil; reduce heat, and simmer 30 minutes. Stir in ½ cup
green onions just before serving. Garnish, if desired. **Yield:** 6 cups.

Lamb Sandwiches

In the past, a leg of
lamb was more likely
to be reserved for
company. Today, Cat
Christianson's Lamb
Sandwiches are the
perfect example of
how lamb fits into
everyday family meals
as well as more formal
menus for Christmas
entertaining.

1 (3- to 4-pound) boneless leg of
  lamb
2 garlic cloves, thinly sliced
1 cup raspberry vinegar
2 tablespoons olive oil
1 tablespoon chopped fresh thyme
2 garlic cloves, pressed
¼ teaspoon salt
¼ teaspoon freshly ground pepper
6 to 8 Sweet Potato Rolls, split (see
  recipe on page 45)
24 small lettuce leaves
Raspberry Mayonnaise

✦ **Cut** small slits in lamb, using a sharp knife; insert garlic slices into slits.

✦ **Combine** raspberry vinegar and next 3 ingredients in a large shallow dish
or heavy-duty, zip-top plastic bag; add lamb. Seal bag; chill 8 hours, turning
lamb occasionally.

✦ **Remove** lamb from marinade, discarding marinade. Sprinkle lamb with salt
and pepper.

✦ **Grill,** covered with grill lid, over high heat (400° to 500°) 30 to 45 minutes
or until a meat thermometer inserted into thickest portion of lamb registers
150° (medium-rare). Cool.

✦ **Cut** lamb into ⅛-inch-thick slices; serve on Sweet Potato Rolls with lettuce
and Raspberry Mayonnaise. **Yield:** 6 to 8 servings.

Raspberry Mayonnaise

¼ cup egg substitute
2 tablespoons raspberry vinegar
¼ teaspoon salt
⅛ teaspoon ground white pepper
¾ cup olive oil or vegetable oil

✦ **Process** first 4 ingredients in a blender or a food processor until blended.
Turn blender on high; add oil in a slow, steady stream; process until mixture is
thickened. Cover and chill. **Yield:** 1⅓ cups.

Cat Christianson
Brevard, North Carolina

Oven-Grilled Reubens

(pictured on page 65)

Here's a new technique for oven-grilled sandwiches and a great way to prepare hot sandwiches for a group. If you use deli meats, sauté them three to five minutes over medium-high heat to remove excess water.

2 cups canned sauerkraut, drained
¾ teaspoon caraway seeds
1¾ cups Thousand Island dressing
12 rye bread slices without caraway
      seeds

6 pumpernickel bread slices
12 (1-ounce) Swiss cheese slices
48 thin slices shaved corned beef
      (about 1½ pounds)

✦ **Stir** together sauerkraut and caraway seeds.
✦ **Spread** Thousand Island dressing evenly on 1 side of bread slices. Layer 6 rye bread slices and 6 pumpernickel bread slices evenly with cheese, sauerkraut mixture, and corned beef. Stack to make 6 (2-layer) sandwiches, ending with remaining rye bread slices.
✦ **Coat** a baking sheet with vegetable cooking spray; arrange sandwiches on baking sheet. Coat bottom of a second baking sheet with cooking spray; place, coated side down, on sandwiches.
✦ **Bake** at 475° for 15 to 20 minutes or until bread is golden and cheese is slightly melted. Serve warm. **Yield:** 6 servings.

Ham and Cheese Melts

Wrap and freeze these tasty sandwiches up to one month before baking. Thaw them in the refrigerator overnight, and bake as directed.

½ cup butter or margarine, softened
1 tablespoon poppy seeds
2 tablespoons minced onion
2 tablespoons Dijon mustard

8 hamburger buns
1 pound thinly sliced cooked ham
8 slices Swiss cheese

✦ **Stir** together first 4 ingredients, stirring well; spread mixture evenly on cut surfaces of buns.
✦ **Arrange** ham evenly on bottom halves of buns; top each with a cheese slice. Cover with top halves of buns. Wrap each sandwich in aluminum foil, and place on a baking sheet.
✦ **Bake** at 350° for 20 minutes or until sandwiches are thoroughly heated. Serve immediately. **Yield:** 8 servings.

Entrées for the Feast

Gather around the holiday table for a memorable meal featuring one of this chapter's exceptional entrées. ✦ Serve Crown Roast of Pork with Stuffing (page 74) or Hazelnut-Crusted Rack of Lamb with Cherry-Wine Sauce (page 73) for an impressive main course. ✦ Create a classic Christmas dinner with succulent Baked Ham with Bourbon Glaze (page 76), or try a twist on tradition with Amelia Barreto's Cuban-style New Year's Turkey (page 83). ✦ From beef tenderloin to grilled quail, these elegant entrées will be the stars of an old-fashioned feast.

New Year's Turkey, page 83

Standing Rib Roast

1 (5- to 6-pound) rib roast (3 ribs)
Steamed new potatoes (optional)
Steamed carrots (optional)

Garnishes: fresh sage sprigs, fresh
rosemary sprigs

+ **Place** roast, fat side up, on a rack in a shallow roasting pan. Insert a meat thermometer into roast, making sure it does not touch fat or bone.
+ **Bake** roast at 350° for 2 hours or until meat thermometer registers 145° (medium-rare) or 160° (medium). Let stand 10 minutes before slicing. If desired, serve with new potatoes and carrots, and garnish. **Yield:** 8 to 10 servings.

Mary Beth House
Chapel Hill, North Carolina

Beef Tenderloin
With Five-Onion Sauce

(pictured on page 150)

(pictured on page 150)

1 (3½-pound) trimmed beef tenderloin
1½ teaspoons salt, divided
1 teaspoon pepper, divided
2 tablespoons canola oil
3 tablespoons butter or margarine
2 large yellow onions, sliced and
    separated into rings

2 large purple onions, sliced and
    separated into rings
2 bunches green onions, chopped
12 shallots, chopped
5 garlic cloves, minced
½ cup cognac
½ cup beef broth

Beverle Grieco hosts an annual holiday dinner for as many as 60 family members and friends. She serves this beef tenderloin along with roasted vegetables, risotto, a mixed green salad, and two decadent desserts (see menu, page 150).

Beverle says, "This menu is perfect because the food is both easy and beautiful. . . . It allows you to enjoy the day of your dinner at a relaxed pace."

+ **Sprinkle** tenderloin with ½ teaspoon salt and ½ teaspoon pepper. Secure with string at 1-inch intervals. Brown tenderloin on all sides in hot oil in a heavy roasting pan or ovenproof Dutch oven. Remove tenderloin, reserving drippings in pan. Add butter to drippings, and cook over medium-high heat until melted. Add yellow and purple onion rings; sauté 5 minutes.
+ **Add** green onions, shallots, and garlic; sauté 10 minutes. Stir in cognac and broth; cook over high heat, stirring constantly, until liquid evaporates (about 5 minutes). Place tenderloin on top.
+ **Bake,** covered, at 400° for 45 minutes or until a meat thermometer inserted into thickest portion of tenderloin registers 145° (medium-rare).
+ **Remove** tenderloin from roasting pan, reserving onion mixture in pan; cover tenderloin loosely, and let stand at room temperature 10 minutes before slicing.
+ **Cook** onion mixture over medium heat, stirring constantly, 3 to 5 minutes or until liquid evaporates. Stir in remaining 1 teaspoon salt and remaining ½ teaspoon pepper. Serve sauce with sliced tenderloin. **Yield:** 8 servings.

Beverle Grieco
Houston, Texas

Beef Tenderloin Steaks
With Balsamic Sauce

(pictured below and on page 150)

4 (6-ounce) beef tenderloin steaks
2 tablespoons coarse-grain sea salt or
    1 tablespoon regular salt
1 tablespoon coarsely ground pepper

2 tablespoons olive oil
Balsamic Sauce
Garnish: fresh thyme sprigs

✦ **Rub** steaks with sea salt and pepper. Cook steaks in hot oil in a large oven-proof skillet over high heat 2 to 3 minutes on each side.

✦ **Bake** at 350° for 8 to 15 minutes or to desired degree of doneness. Serve with Balsamic Sauce. Garnish, if desired. **Yield:** 4 servings.

Balsamic Sauce

¼ cup dry red wine
¼ cup dry sherry
3 tablespoons balsamic vinegar
2 garlic cloves, chopped

1 shallot, chopped
2 egg yolks
⅓ cup unsalted butter, melted

✦ **Bring** first 5 ingredients to a boil in a small saucepan; cook 2 minutes. Cool.

✦ **Whisk** yolks into wine mixture; cook over low heat, whisking constantly, until thickened. Slowly whisk in butter until blended. Serve sauce immediately. **Yield:** ½ cup.

Sheri Castle
Raleigh, North Carolina

For Sheri Castle and her husband, Doug Tidwell, Christmas dinner is an elegant and intimate occasion. They share an elaborately set table with their three-year-old daughter, Lily, who has already acquired a keen taste for sauces. This recipe, developed over several holiday seasons, is one of Lily's favorites.

Peppered Rib-Eye Steaks

¾ teaspoon freshly ground black
   pepper
1 teaspoon dried thyme
1½ teaspoons garlic powder
½ teaspoon salt

½ teaspoon ground red pepper
½ teaspoon lemon pepper
½ teaspoon dried parsley flakes
2 (1½-inch-thick) rib-eye steaks
1 tablespoon olive oil

✦ **Stir** together first 7 ingredients. Brush steaks with oil; rub with pepper
mixture. Cover and chill 1 hour.
✦ **Grill,** covered with grill lid, over medium-high heat (350° to 400°) about
10 minutes on each side or to desired degree of doneness. **Yield:** 2 servings.

Sandi Pichon
Slidell, Louisiana

Herb-Peppered Veal Chops

4 (1½- to 2-inch-thick) veal chops
   (about 3½ pounds)
2 tablespoons vegetable oil, divided
2 garlic cloves, minced
2 teaspoons paprika
1½ teaspoons dried thyme
1½ teaspoons dried oregano
¾ teaspoon salt
¾ teaspoon ground cumin

¾ teaspoon lemon pepper
1 teaspoon ground black pepper
¾ teaspoon ground red pepper
1 (14½-ounce) can beef broth
1 tablespoon cornstarch
2 tablespoons water
¼ teaspoon Worcestershire sauce
Garnish: roasted whole shallots

✦ **Brush** chops with 1 tablespoon oil, and rub with garlic.
✦ **Stir** together paprika and next 7 ingredients in a small bowl. Rub over
chops. Cover and chill 1 hour.
✦ **Heat** remaining 1 tablespoon oil in a large ovenproof skillet over medium-
high heat. Cook chops in hot oil 3 minutes on each side or until browned.
✦ **Bake** at 350° for 20 minutes or until done. Remove chops from skillet,
reserving drippings in skillet; keep chops warm.
✦ **Add** broth to reserved drippings, stirring to loosen particles; bring to a boil.
Boil until reduced to 1 cup (about 10 minutes); skim fat from broth mixture.
✦ **Stir** together cornstarch, 2 tablespoons water, and Worcestershire sauce.
Gradually stir into broth mixture; bring to a boil. Boil, stirring constantly,
1 minute. Serve sauce with chops. Garnish, if desired. **Yield:** 4 servings.

Robin Andrews
Morristown, Tennessee

Hazelnut-Crusted Rack of Lamb With Cherry-Wine Sauce

¼ cup coarse-grained Dijon mustard
2 (8-rib) lamb rib roasts (2¾ to 3 pounds each), trimmed
⅓ cup fine, dry breadcrumbs
⅓ cup finely chopped hazelnuts
¼ cup finely chopped fresh parsley

1 tablespoon chopped fresh thyme or 1 teaspoon dried thyme
½ teaspoon freshly ground pepper
¼ teaspoon salt
Cherry-Wine Sauce

◆ **Spread** mustard over lamb roasts. Stir together breadcrumbs and next 5 ingredients; pat over roasts.
◆ **Place** roasts in a lightly greased roasting pan, fat side out and ribs criss-crossed. Insert a meat thermometer into thickest portion of lamb, making sure it does not touch fat or bone.
◆ **Bake** at 400° for 10 minutes. Remove from oven; cool slightly. Shield exposed bones with strips of aluminum foil to prevent excessive browning. Reduce heat to 375°; bake 35 more minutes or until meat thermometer registers 150° (medium-rare). Let stand 10 minutes before slicing. Serve with Cherry-Wine Sauce. **Yield:** 5 to 8 servings.

Cherry-Wine Sauce

⅔ cup dry red wine
⅓ cup beef broth
3 tablespoons honey
1½ teaspoons chopped fresh thyme or ½ teaspoon dried thyme
¼ teaspoon salt

¼ teaspoon dry mustard
2 teaspoons cornstarch
2 tablespoons balsamic vinegar
1 (16½-ounce) can pitted dark cherries, drained

◆ **Stir** together first 6 ingredients in a heavy saucepan; bring to a boil. Boil 5 minutes.
◆ **Combine** cornstarch and balsamic vinegar, stirring well; add to wine mixture. Bring to a boil over medium-high heat; boil 1 minute. Stir in cherries. **Yield:** 1½ cups.

Lynda Maksin
Farmington, Missouri

"I have always enjoyed lamb at restaurants, so I decided to give rack of lamb a try. Happily, assembling the recipe was easy. When the delicious aroma wafted through the kitchen, I felt great about my choice. We now have a new Christmas tradition."
—Lynda Maksin

Crown Roast of Pork with Stuffing

*This impressive entrée, with its savory sausage stuffing, could be
the highlight of your Christmas dinner. To carve, remove the stuffing
from the center of the roast. Using a carving fork to secure the roast,
slice down between the ribs, and remove one chop at a time.*

1 (16-rib) crown roast of pork (about
   8 pounds)
3 tablespoons vegetable oil, divided
¾ teaspoon salt
¼ teaspoon pepper
3½ pounds baking potatoes, peeled
   and cubed (about 7 medium)
½ teaspoon salt
1 pound sweet Italian sausage, casings
   removed

5 celery ribs, finely chopped (about
   2 cups)
4 carrots, scraped and finely chopped
   (about 2 cups)
3 large onions, chopped (about 4 cups)
2 garlic cloves, minced
⅓ cup chopped fresh parsley
1 teaspoon fennel seeds, crushed
¾ teaspoon salt
⅛ teaspoon pepper

✦ **Brush** roast with 1 tablespoon oil; sprinkle with ¾ teaspoon salt and ¼ teaspoon pepper. Place roast, bone ends up, in a lightly greased shallow roasting pan. Insert a meat thermometer into roast, making sure it does not touch fat or bone.

✦ **Bake** at 475° for 15 minutes. Reduce oven temperature to 325°, and bake 1 hour and 30 minutes.

✦ **Combine** potato, ½ teaspoon salt, and water to cover in a large saucepan. Bring to a boil; cover, reduce heat, and simmer 10 minutes or until potato is tender. Drain.

✦ **Brown** sausage in a large skillet, stirring until it crumbles. Remove from skillet with a slotted spoon, reserving drippings in skillet. Add remaining 2 tablespoons oil to drippings.

✦ **Add** celery and next 3 ingredients to skillet; cook, stirring constantly, 15 minutes or until tender.

✦ **Stir** in potato, sausage, parsley, and remaining 3 ingredients.

✦ **Spoon** about 3 cups stuffing mixture into cavity of roast, mounding slightly. Cover stuffing and exposed ends of ribs with aluminum foil. Spoon remaining stuffing mixture into a lightly greased 11- x 7-inch baking dish; cover with foil.

✦ **Bake** roast and stuffing at 325° for 30 minutes or until meat thermometer registers 160°. Remove roast from oven, and let stand, covered, 10 minutes before slicing. Bake stuffing in baking dish 15 more minutes. **Yield:** 8 servings.

Apple-Stuffed Tenderloin with Praline-Mustard Glaze

¼ cup raisins
⅓ cup bourbon or apple juice
2 (¾- to 1-pound) pork tenderloins
1 cooking apple, thinly sliced
1 onion, thinly sliced

2 or 3 garlic cloves, halved
1 tablespoon chopped fresh rosemary
¼ cup maple syrup
2 tablespoons dark brown sugar
2 tablespoons prepared mustard

✦ **Combine** raisins and bourbon in a bowl; let stand 1 hour.
✦ **Cut** pork tenderloins lengthwise down center, cutting to, but not through, bottom. Alternate apple and onion slices down centers of tenderloins. Top evenly with raisins, garlic, and rosemary. Close tenderloins over filling; tie at 1-inch intervals. Place on sheets of heavy-duty aluminum foil.
✦ **Stir** together syrup, sugar, and mustard; brush half of glaze over tenderloins. Close foil, and fold to seal. Place in a 13- x 9-inch pan.
✦ **Bake** at 325° for 25 minutes. Open foil; brush tenderloins with remaining glaze. Close foil, and bake 20 to 25 more minutes or until a meat thermometer inserted into thickest portion registers 160°. **Yield:** 6 servings.

Jane C. Clemence
Amarillo, Texas

Your family will devour Jane Clemence's delicious stuffed pork. Apple slices, onion, garlic, rosemary, and bourbon-plumped raisins make up the flavorful stuffing, and the sweet mustard glaze adds moisture.

Pork Medaillons in Mustard Sauce

3 tablespoons vegetable oil
1 tablespoon coarse-grained mustard
½ teaspoon salt
½ teaspoon pepper

2 (¾-pound) pork tenderloins
¼ cup dry white wine
Mustard Sauce
Garnish: fresh basil sprigs

✦ **Stir** together first 4 ingredients; rub over pork tenderloins. Place in a large heavy-duty, zip-top plastic bag; seal bag, and marinate in refrigerator 8 hours.
✦ **Place** tenderloins on a lightly greased rack in a shallow roasting pan. Insert a meat thermometer into thickest part of 1 tenderloin. Bake at 400° for 25 minutes or until thermometer registers 160°, basting every 10 minutes with wine.
✦ **Slice** tenderloins into ¾-inch slices; arrange slices evenly on dinner plates. Spoon Mustard Sauce around slices. Garnish, if desired. **Yield:** 4 servings.

Mustard Sauce

1¾ cups whipping cream
¼ cup coarse-grained mustard

¼ teaspoon salt
⅛ teaspoon ground white pepper

✦ **Cook** whipping cream in a heavy saucepan over medium heat, stirring often, until reduced to 1¼ cups (about 15 minutes). Do not boil. Stir in mustard, salt, and pepper; cook, stirring constantly, 1 minute. **Yield:** 1¼ cups.

Baked Ham with Bourbon Glaze

1 cup honey
½ cup molasses
½ cup bourbon
¼ cup orange juice

2 tablespoons Dijon mustard
1 (6- to 8-pound) smoked ham half
Garnish: fresh herb sprigs

✦ **Place** honey and molasses in a 1-quart microwave-safe dish. Microwave at HIGH 1 minute; whisk to blend. Whisk in bourbon, juice, and mustard.

✦ **Remove** skin and excess fat from ham; place ham in a roasting pan. Bake, uncovered, at 325° on lower oven rack for 1 hour and 30 minutes or until a meat thermometer inserted into thickest portion registers 140°, basting occasionally with glaze. Let stand 10 minutes before slicing. Bring drippings and remaining glaze to a boil in a saucepan. Remove from heat; serve with ham. Garnish, if desired. **Yield:** 12 to 14 servings.

Roevis McKay
New York, New York

Shrimp Lafayette

Serve this spicy seafood dish with a mixed greens salad and crusty French bread for a simple, yet elegant, holiday meal.

1¼ pounds unpeeled medium-size
    fresh shrimp
2 cups water
1 teaspoon salt, divided
½ teaspoon ground black pepper,
    divided
2 tablespoons butter or margarine,
    melted and divided
2 medium-size red bell peppers,
    chopped (2 cups)

1 large onion, chopped (1 cup)
1 tablespoon seeded and chopped
    jalapeño pepper
4 medium tomatoes, peeled, seeded,
    and chopped (4 cups)
¼ teaspoon brown sugar
¼ teaspoon ground red pepper
⅛ teaspoon ground white pepper
2 garlic cloves, chopped
Hot cooked linguine

✦ **Peel** shrimp, reserving shells. Devein shrimp, if desired. Set shrimp aside.

✦ **Combine** shrimp shells, 2 cups water, ½ teaspoon salt, and ¼ teaspoon black pepper in a medium saucepan; bring to a boil. Reduce heat, and simmer, uncovered, 15 minutes. Pour mixture through a wire-mesh strainer into a bowl, discarding shells. Set aside ¼ cup shrimp stock. Reserve remaining shrimp stock for another use, if desired.

✦ **Cook** shrimp in 1 tablespoon butter in a large saucepan over medium-high heat, stirring constantly, 3 minutes or until shrimp turn pink. Remove shrimp from pan; set aside, and keep warm.

✦ **Cook** red bell pepper, onion, and jalapeño pepper in remaining 1 table-spoon butter in pan over medium-high heat, stirring constantly, 5 minutes or until vegetables are tender. Stir in remaining ½ teaspoon salt, remaining ¼ teaspoon black pepper, tomato, and next 4 ingredients; cook 5 minutes, stirring occasionally.

✦ **Add** reserved shrimp stock; cook 5 minutes, stirring occasionally. Add shrimp; cook until mixture is thoroughly heated, stirring occasionally. Serve over linguine. **Yield:** 4 servings.

Bouchées aux Fruits de Mer

Nancy Guillemart grew up all over the South, but she now calls France home. Nancy and her mother-in-law, Marcelle, cook together—both Southern and French cuisines.

"Cooking has been our common language," says Nancy, "because Marcelle does not speak English."

Here is one of Nancy's best-loved flavors of her new home.

1 (10-ounce) package puff pastry shells
4 fresh parsley sprigs
3 fresh thyme sprigs
1 bay leaf
5 tablespoons butter or margarine, divided
1 pound peeled medium-size fresh shrimp, halved
12 sea scallops, halved (1 pound)
18 peeled crawfish tails, halved (¾ pound)

1½ cups dry white wine, divided
2 tablespoons all-purpose flour
2 shallots, minced
¼ pound fresh mushrooms, chopped
1 (8-ounce) jar clam juice
⅓ cup all-purpose flour
1 egg yolk, lightly beaten
1 (8-ounce) container sour cream
¼ teaspoon salt
½ teaspoon pepper
Garnish: chopped fresh parsley

✦ **Bake** pastry shells according to package directions. Set aside.

✦ **Place** herbs on a 6-inch square of cheesecloth; tie with string. Set aside.

✦ **Melt** 2 tablespoons butter in a large skillet over medium heat; add shrimp, scallops, and crawfish; sauté 4 minutes or until done.

✦ **Stir** in ½ cup wine and 2 tablespoons flour, and cook, stirring occasionally, 5 minutes. Remove seafood sauce from skillet; set aside.

✦ **Melt** 1 tablespoon butter in a Dutch oven over medium heat; add shallots and mushrooms, and sauté until tender. Stir in remaining 1 cup wine and herb bag. Bring to a boil. Stir in clam juice; cook until liquid is reduced to 1½ cups (about 15 to 20 minutes). Discard herb bag.

✦ **Melt** remaining 2 tablespoons butter in skillet over medium heat; stir in ⅓ cup flour until smooth. Cook, stirring constantly, 1 minute. Gradually stir into mushroom mixture. Combine yolk and sour cream. Add to mushroom mixture; cook over low heat, stirring constantly, 5 minutes. Stir in salt and pepper. Spoon into pastry shells; top with seafood sauce. Garnish, if desired. **Yield:** 6 servings.

Nancy Guillemart
Saumur, France

Easy Oven-Roasted Chicken

1 (3- to 4-pound) broiler-fryer
6 garlic cloves, peeled
½ teaspoon salt
½ teaspoon pepper

1 (14½-ounce) can chicken broth
1 (1.61-ounce) package brown
   gravy mix

✦ **Place** chicken, breast side up, in a lightly greased shallow roasting pan. Place garlic in chicken cavity. Sprinkle cavity and outside of chicken evenly with salt and pepper. Pour chicken broth over chicken.

✦ **Bake,** uncovered, at 400° for 55 to 60 minutes or until a meat thermometer inserted into thigh registers 180°, basting often with chicken broth. Remove chicken to a serving plate, reserving drippings. Remove garlic from chicken, and mash.

✦ **Pour** drippings through a wire-mesh strainer into a 2-cup liquid measuring cup. Add enough water to measure 2 cups. Pour into a medium saucepan. Whisk in mashed garlic and gravy mix. Bring mixture to a boil over medium-high heat, stirring constantly. Reduce heat, and simmer, stirring constantly, 10 minutes or until thickened. Serve with chicken. **Yield:** 4 to 6 servings.

Greek Chicken Breasts

4 bone-in chicken breast halves
8 garlic cloves, pressed
2 tablespoons olive oil
1 teaspoon salt
1 teaspoon freshly ground pepper
2 tablespoons chopped fresh oregano
   or 2 teaspoons dried oregano

4 lemons, thinly sliced
16 to 20 kalamata olives, pitted
1 (4-ounce) package crumbled feta
   cheese
Garnishes: lemon slices, fresh oregano
   sprigs

✦ **Lift** skin gently from chicken breasts without detaching it; place 2 garlic cloves under skin of each chicken breast. Replace skin.

✦ **Rub** breasts evenly with oil; sprinkle with salt, pepper, and chopped oregano.

✦ **Place** lemon slices in a 13- x 9-inch baking dish, and arrange chicken breasts over lemon. Sprinkle olives around chicken.

✦ **Bake,** uncovered, at 350° for 45 minutes or until done. Remove from oven, and sprinkle with feta cheese. Garnish, if desired. **Yield:** 4 servings.

Caramelized Chicken
With Cranberry Conserve

3 tablespoons frozen orange juice concentrate, thawed and undiluted
2 tablespoons balsamic vinegar
2 tablespoons dry sherry
1 garlic clove, minced
4 skinned and boned chicken breast halves
3 tablespoons brown sugar
1 tablespoon dark sesame oil
1 small onion, chopped
½ cup dried cranberries
1 to 2 tablespoons sesame seeds, toasted (optional)
1 to 2 tablespoons minced green onions (optional)
Garnish: green onion fans

✦ **Combine** first 4 ingredients in a heavy-duty, zip-top plastic bag; add chicken. Seal and chill at least 1 hour. Remove chicken, reserving marinade.
✦ **Cook** sugar and sesame oil in a large nonstick skillet over medium-high heat, stirring constantly, 4 minutes. Add chicken; cook 3 minutes on each side.
✦ **Add** reserved marinade, onion, and cranberries; cook, stirring and turning chicken often, 10 minutes or until chicken is done. Remove chicken; let stand 5 minutes. Slice chicken; serve with cranberry mixture. If desired, sprinkle with sesame seeds and green onions, and garnish. **Yield:** 4 servings.

Janice Elder
Charlotte, North Carolina

Imperial Chicken

4 cups soft breadcrumbs

½ cup grated Parmesan cheese

2 tablespoons paprika

½ cup dried parsley flakes

1½ teaspoons garlic powder

1½ teaspoons salt

1½ teaspoons pepper

12 skinned and boned chicken breast halves

1 cup butter or margarine, melted

✦ **Stir** together first 7 ingredients in a shallow dish. Dip chicken in butter; dredge in breadcrumb mixture. Place in 2 lightly greased 15- x 10-inch jellyroll pans. Bake at 350° for 30 to 35 minutes or until done. **Yield:** 12 servings.

Carolyn Bond
Knoxville, Tennessee

Orange-Ginger Hens
With Cranberry Salsa

(pictured on page 151)

4 (1½-pound) Cornish hens

1 teaspoon salt

½ teaspoon pepper

¼ cup butter or margarine

¼ cup lemon juice

1 tablespoon grated orange rind

¾ cup fresh orange juice

4 garlic cloves, minced

1 tablespoon grated fresh ginger

1 tablespoon Dijon mustard

1 teaspoon prepared horseradish

Cranberry Salsa

Hot cooked basmati rice pilaf (optional)

✦ **Rub** hens with salt and pepper; tie ends of legs together, if desired. Place, breast side up, on a rack in a roasting pan. Bring butter and next 7 ingredients to a boil in a saucepan; pour over hens. Bake at 375° for 1 hour or until done, basting often with butter mixture. Serve with salsa and, if desired, pilaf. **Yield:** 4 servings.

Cranberry Salsa

1 cup dried cranberries

½ cup fresh orange juice

½ cup peeled, seeded, and diced cucumber

½ cup diced purple onion

¼ cup chopped fresh cilantro

1 garlic clove, minced

1 jalapeño pepper, seeded and diced

¼ cup fresh lime juice

½ teaspoon ground cumin

½ teaspoon salt

✦ **Soak** cranberries in orange juice in a bowl 30 minutes. Stir in cucumber and remaining ingredients. Cover and chill. **Yield:** 3 cups.

Miriam Baroga
Fircrest, Washington

Cornish Hens with Barley-Mushroom Stuffing

June MacIvor collected recipes during her years as a military wife. She and her husband have lived in 19 different houses—and she can still describe every kitchen.

June says, "My hope for my daughter and grandchildren is that preparing and sharing food will be as important for them as it has been for me." Here, she shares one of her family's cherished holiday recipes.

3 (1½-pound) Cornish hens
⅓ cup soy sauce
1½ tablespoons honey
1½ tablespoons dry sherry
½ teaspoon garlic powder
1 cup uncooked barley

2½ cups chicken broth
1½ cups chopped fresh mushrooms
¾ cup chopped water chestnuts
4 green onions, chopped
Garnish: green onions

◆ **Place** hens in a large heavy-duty, zip-top plastic bag.
◆ **Stir** together soy sauce and next 3 ingredients; pour into cavities and over hens. Seal bag; chill, turning often, 3 to 4 hours.
◆ **Bring** barley and chicken broth to a boil in a saucepan; cover, reduce heat, and simmer 45 minutes or until liquid is absorbed. Remove from heat; stir in mushrooms, water chestnuts, and chopped green onions.
◆ **Remove** hens from marinade, reserving marinade. Bring marinade to a boil in a small saucepan; set aside. Stuff hen cavities with barley mixture, reserving extra mixture. Place hens, breast side up, on a rack in a shallow roasting pan.
◆ **Bake** hens at 375° for 1 hour and 30 minutes or until a meat thermometer inserted into meaty part of thigh registers 180° and inserted into stuffing registers 165°, basting hens occasionally with reserved marinade. Serve with reserved barley mixture. Garnish, if desired. **Yield:** 3 servings.

June MacIvor
Clarkesville, Georgia

New Year's Turkey

(pictured on page 68)

1 (10- to 12-pound) turkey
2 tablespoons salt
1 tablespoon pepper
⅓ cup balsamic vinegar
1 tablespoon minced fresh garlic
2 tablespoons olive oil
⅔ cup butter or margarine
½ cup chopped onion
1 pound ground veal
½ pound ground boiled ham
6 white bread slices
1 cup milk
1 large egg, lightly beaten

1 cup chopped apple
1 tablespoon Cajun seasoning
1 teaspoon salt
1 teaspoon pepper
1 cup raisins
½ cup chopped walnuts
½ cup minced fresh parsley
1 cup chopped onion
1½ cups sweet vermouth
½ cup honey
Garnishes: fresh parsley sprigs,
            kumquat leaves, kumquats

> "My family loves the traditional American holiday meals, but we always add a Cuban twist. For instance, my stuffing for this turkey is a rich mixture of veal, ham, raisins, apples, and walnuts."
>
> —Amelia Barreto

✦ **Remove** giblets and neck from turkey, and reserve for another use. Rinse turkey with cold water, and pat dry. Place turkey in a large shallow dish. Stir together 2 tablespoons salt and next 4 ingredients; pour over turkey. Cover and chill at least 6 hours.

✦ **Melt** butter in a large skillet. Add ½ cup chopped onion; sauté until tender. Add veal and ham; cook over medium heat, stirring often, 5 minutes. Remove from heat.

✦ **Remove** and discard crusts from bread; tear bread into small pieces. Combine breadcrumbs, milk, and egg in a large bowl; stir in apple and next 6 ingredients. Stir in veal mixture.

✦ **Remove** turkey from refrigerator, and brush turkey cavity with marinade. Spoon stuffing into turkey cavity; truss turkey, using string. Lift wingtips up and over back, and tuck them under bird. Place turkey, breast side up, in a large roasting pan.

✦ **Cover** turkey with aluminum foil, and bake at 400° for 30 minutes. Reduce heat to 350°, and bake 2 hours, basting occasionally with pan drippings.

✦ **Process** 1 cup onion, vermouth, and honey in an electric blender until smooth. Pour mixture over turkey; bake 1 more hour or until a meat thermometer inserted into turkey thigh registers 180° and inserted into stuffing registers 165°.

✦ **Broil** turkey 5 inches from heat (with electric oven door partially open) until golden. Garnish, if desired. **Yield:** 10 to 12 servings.

Amelia Barreto
Bonita Beach, Florida

Wild Rice-Stuffed
Turkey Breast, below;
Roasted Winter
Vegetables, page 97

Wild Rice-Stuffed Turkey Breast

(pictured above and on page 151)

1 (3-ounce) package dried
   cherries
1½ cups port wine
3½ cups chicken broth, divided
½ cup uncooked wild rice
½ cup uncooked long-grain rice
1 teaspoon freshly ground pepper
1 small onion, chopped
½ cup diced celery

2 cups soft whole wheat breadcrumbs
1 (6-pound) bone-in turkey breast,
   deboned*
2 teaspoons chopped fresh rosemary
2 garlic cloves, minced
1 tablespoon kosher salt
1 tablespoon freshly ground pepper
2 tablespoons butter or margarine
¼ cup all-purpose flour

✦ **Combine** cherries and wine; let stand 1 hour. Drain, reserving wine.
✦ **Bring** 2 cups broth and next 5 ingredients to a boil in a medium saucepan;
cover, reduce heat, and simmer 30 minutes or until liquid is absorbed and rice
is tender. Cool; stir in breadcrumbs and cherries.

✦ **Place** turkey between 2 sheets of heavy-duty plastic wrap; flatten to 1-inch thickness, using a meat mallet or rolling pin.

✦ **Rub** skinless side of turkey with rosemary and garlic; spread evenly with rice mixture. Starting at a long side, tightly roll up breast, jellyroll fashion; secure at 2-inch intervals with kitchen string.

✦ **Sprinkle** turkey with salt and 1 tablespoon pepper; place on a lightly greased rack in a roasting pan.

✦ **Bake** at 375° for 1 hour and 45 minutes or until a meat thermometer inserted into thickest portion registers 170°. Remove from pan, reserving any drippings in pan; let turkey stand 10 minutes before slicing.

✦ **Melt** butter in a heavy saucepan over low heat; stir in reserved drippings. Whisk flour into butter until mixture is smooth. Cook, whisking constantly, 1 minute. Gradually add reserved wine and remaining 1½ cups broth; cook over medium heat, whisking occasionally, 5 minutes or until thickened. Serve with sliced stuffed turkey. **Yield:** 8 to 10 servings.

*A 6-pound bone-in turkey breast yields approximately a 4¾-pound boneless turkey breast. Save yourself time by having your butcher debone the turkey breast for you. Just call your supermarket ahead of time. If a fresh turkey is not available, be sure to allow time for the butcher to thaw a frozen turkey.

Grilled Quail with
Red Wine-Blackberry Sauce

2 (14-ounce) packages quail,
    dressed with breasts deboned
1 (8-ounce) bottle Italian dressing
½ cup dry red wine

1 (9.5-ounce) jar seedless blackberry
    spread (we tested with
    Dickinson's)

✦ **Rinse** quail with cold water, and pat dry. Place in a large shallow dish or large heavy-duty, zip-top plastic bag; add Italian dressing. Cover or seal; chill 8 hours. Remove quail, discarding marinade.

✦ **Cook** wine in a small saucepan over medium heat 5 minutes or until reduced by half. Whisk in blackberry spread until smooth. Reserve ¾ cup.

✦ **Grill** quail over medium heat (300° to 350°) 15 minutes or until done, turning once and basting with remaining blackberry sauce. Serve with reserved ¾ cup sauce. **Yield:** 4 servings.

Philip Palmer
Athens, Georgia

Seasonal Sides and Salads

Complete your Christmas feast with trimmings that are as much a tradition as turkey. ✦ Turn to page 88 for two versions of a holiday must-have: dressing. Try Glenda LaRocca's spicy Creole Dressing for a taste of New Orleans, or save some time with easy Sweet Cornbread Dressing. ✦ Other side dishes that the season seems to require follow, including giblet gravy, cranberry relish, brussels sprouts, and corn pudding. ✦ Sensational salads start on page 99 and provide plenty of Southern favorites, from Congealed Cherry Salad to Spicy Potato Salad.

Roasted Asparagus with Red Pepper Sauce, page 92;
Pistachio Risotto with Saffron, page 91

Creole Dressing

1 (16-ounce) container chicken livers, drained
1 (10-ounce) container fresh oysters, undrained
½ (16-ounce) loaf day-old French bread, crumbled
½ cup butter or margarine
5 celery ribs, chopped
4 garlic cloves, minced
2 bunches green onions, chopped
2 large onions, chopped
1 cup chopped fresh parsley
½ pound ground beef, cooked and drained
½ pound ground pork, cooked and drained
1 teaspoon rubbed sage
1 teaspoon ground thyme
½ teaspoon pepper
2 tablespoons Creole seasoning

✦ **Chop** chicken livers; cook in boiling water until tender. Drain; set aside.

✦ **Drain** oysters, reserving liquid; coarsely chop oysters. Place bread in a bowl. Pour reserved liquid over bread; set aside.

✦ **Melt** butter in a large skillet over medium-high heat; add celery and next 4 ingredients. Cook, stirring constantly, until vegetables are tender. Add livers, oysters, bread mixture, beef, and remaining ingredients. Reduce heat; simmer, uncovered, about 15 minutes. Spoon into a lightly greased 13- x 9-inch baking dish. Bake at 350° for 30 minutes or until heated. **Yield:** 10 servings.

Glenda LaRocca
Houston, Texas

Sweet Cornbread Dressing

(pictured on page 154)

2 (8½-ounce) packages corn muffin mix
2 celery ribs, chopped
1 medium onion, chopped
2 tablespoons vegetable oil
1 (10¾-ounce) can cream of chicken soup, undiluted
1 (14½-ounce) can chicken broth
1½ teaspoons rubbed sage
½ teaspoon pepper
¼ teaspoon celery salt
2 hard-cooked eggs, chopped

✦ **Prepare** corn muffin mixes according to package directions; pour all batter into a lightly greased 8-inch square pan. Bake at 400° for 25 to 28 minutes or until golden; cool in pan on wire racks. Crumble cornbread into a large bowl.

✦ **Sauté** celery and onion in hot oil in a large skillet until tender. Add soup and next 4 ingredients to skillet, stirring mixture until blended; bring to a boil. Pour over cornbread, stirring until moistened. Stir in chopped egg. Spoon into a lightly greased 8-inch square baking dish. Bake dressing at 350° for 40 to 45 minutes or until lightly browned. **Yield:** 6 to 8 servings.

Margaret McNeil
Memphis, Tennessee

Vidalia Onion and Giblet Gravy

Giblets and neck bone from turkey or
    chicken
1 celery rib, chopped
1 carrot, scraped and chopped
4 black peppercorns
1 whole clove
5 cups chicken broth
4 cups diced Vidalia onion (3 pounds)

¼ cup butter, melted
2 tablespoons peanut oil
¼ cup cornstarch
½ cup heavy whipping cream
Pan drippings from roasted turkey or
    chicken
Salt and pepper

✦ **Combine** first 6 ingredients in a large saucepan. Bring to a boil; cover, reduce heat, and simmer 45 minutes. Pour mixture through a wire-mesh strainer into a bowl; discard celery, carrot, peppercorns, and clove. Remove meat from neck; finely chop neck meat and giblets.

✦ **Cook** onion in butter and oil in a large Dutch oven over medium-high heat, stirring constantly, until onion is lightly browned and tender. Sprinkle cornstarch over onion; cook, stirring constantly, 2 minutes. Add strained broth.

✦ **Cook** mixture over medium-high heat, stirring constantly with a wire whisk, until thickened and bubbly. Stir in neck meat, giblets, and whipping cream.

✦ **Skim** fat from pan drippings; discard fat. Stir pan drippings into gravy. Cook over low heat, stirring constantly, until thoroughly heated. Add salt and pepper to taste. **Yield:** 6 cups.

Cranberry Chutney

½ medium onion, chopped
1 garlic clove, minced
½ jalapeño pepper, seeded and
    chopped
1 (½-inch-thick) slice fresh ginger,
    peeled and chopped
2 tablespoons white wine
    vinegar

½ teaspoon grated lime
    rind
1 tablespoon fresh lime
    juice
2 (16-ounce) cans whole-berry
    cranberry sauce
¼ cup sugar

✦ **Stir** together first 7 ingredients in a medium saucepan.

✦ **Cook** mixture over medium-high heat, stirring constantly, 10 to 15 minutes or until tender.

✦ **Stir** cranberry sauce and sugar into saucepan; bring mixture to a boil. Remove from heat.

✦ **Cover** and chill 2 hours. Store chutney in refrigerator up to 2 weeks. **Yield:** 3½ cups.

Mary Jane Loper
Los Angeles, California

············· ✦ ·············

Mary Jane Loper may live on the West Coast, but she still clings to her Mississippi roots. "Over 15 years ago," she says, "my son and I started the Mississippi Picnic. It's grown to include over 200 people and is held each October."

She developed this recipe several years ago when she couldn't find fresh cranberries.

Tipsy Cranberry Relish

4 cups fresh or frozen cranberries,
    thawed
1½ cups sugar

⅓ to ½ cup brandy or orange juice
½ cup chopped walnuts

✦ **Combine** cranberries and sugar in a 1½-quart microwave-safe casserole; microwave at MEDIUM (50% power) 12 to 13 minutes, stirring once.
✦ **Stir** in brandy and walnuts; cool. Cover; chill 2 to 3 hours. **Yield:** 2½ cups.

Holiday Rice

1¼ cups uncooked long-grain rice
¼ cup butter or margarine,
    melted
1 cup chopped celery
4 green onions, sliced
1 (14½-ounce) can beef broth

1 (4-ounce) can sliced mushrooms,
    undrained
1 tablespoon chopped fresh parsley
1 teaspoon Beau Monde seasoning
¼ to ½ teaspoon dried tarragon
1 bay leaf

✦ **Stir** together first 4 ingredients in a 13- x 9-inch baking dish. Stir in broth and remaining ingredients.
✦ **Bake,** covered, at 350° for 50 minutes, stirring occasionally. Discard bay leaf. **Yield:** 6 to 8 servings.

George Hearne III
Shreveport, Louisiana

Pistachio Risotto with Saffron

(pictured on pages 86 and 150)

¼ cup unsalted butter
1 medium-size yellow onion, chopped
1 teaspoon saffron threads
1¾ cups uncooked Arborio rice

1 cup dry white vermouth or chicken broth
5 cups chicken broth
1 cup grated Parmesan cheese
¼ cup coarsely chopped red pistachios
Garnish: chopped red pistachios

✦ **Melt** butter in a skillet over medium-high heat; add onion. Sauté 5 minutes. Add saffron; sauté 1 minute. Add rice; cook, stirring constantly, 2 minutes. Reduce heat to medium; add vermouth and 2 cups broth. Cook, stirring constantly, until liquid is absorbed.

✦ **Repeat** procedure with remaining 3 cups broth, ½ cup at a time. (Cooking time is 30 to 45 minutes.) Remove from heat; stir in cheese and ¼ cup pistachios. Garnish, if desired. **Yield:** 8 cups.

Beverle Grieco
Houston, Texas

Cracked Pepper Linguine

This simple recipe consists of sautéing onion and garlic and tossing pasta with a handful of sauce ingredients.

8 ounces uncooked dried linguine
1 tablespoon butter or margarine
¼ cup minced onion
2 garlic cloves, pressed
1 (8-ounce) container sour cream

1 tablespoon milk
2 to 3 teaspoons cracked pepper
2 tablespoons grated Parmesan cheese
2 tablespoons chopped fresh parsley
Garnish: fresh parsley sprigs

✦ **Cook** pasta according to package directions; keep warm.
✦ **Melt** butter in a small skillet over medium-high heat; add onion and garlic, and sauté until crisp-tender. Remove mixture from heat, and cool slightly.
✦ **Stir** in sour cream, milk, and pepper. Toss with pasta. Sprinkle with cheese and chopped parsley. Garnish, if desired. **Yield:** 4 servings.

Lemon Linguine: Substitute 1 tablespoon fresh lemon juice for milk. Decrease pepper to ½ teaspoon, and add 1 tablespoon grated lemon rind.

Roasted Asparagus with Red Pepper Sauce

(pictured on pages 86 and 150)

3 tablespoons olive oil
2 tablespoons balsamic vinegar
1 tablespoon teriyaki sauce
1 tablespoon dried basil
½ teaspoon salt
½ teaspoon pepper
¼ teaspoon dry mustard
¼ teaspoon ground nutmeg
1½ pounds fresh asparagus, trimmed
Red Pepper Sauce
Garnish: orange zest

✦ **Stir** together first 8 ingredients in an 11- x 7-inch baking dish. Add asparagus, and toss to coat.

✦ **Bake,** covered, at 375° for 35 minutes, turning asparagus once. Remove with a slotted spoon; serve with Red Pepper Sauce. Garnish, if desired. **Yield:** 6 servings.

Red Pepper Sauce

1 (7-ounce) jar roasted sweet red peppers, drained and sliced
½ small onion, chopped
1 garlic clove, minced
2 tablespoons olive oil
1 tablespoon balsamic vinegar
1 tablespoon orange marmalade
1 tablespoon teriyaki sauce
¼ teaspoon dry mustard
¼ teaspoon ground nutmeg
⅛ teaspoon dried crushed red pepper
¼ cup mayonnaise

✦ **Sauté** first 3 ingredients in hot oil in a large skillet over medium-high heat 2 minutes. Add vinegar and next 5 ingredients; cook 3 minutes. Remove from heat; stir in mayonnaise. **Yield:** 1¼ cups.

Devon Delaney
Princeton, New Jersey

Buttered Asparagus Spears

(pictured on page 151)

3 pounds fresh asparagus*
2 quarts water
¼ cup butter or margarine
½ teaspoon salt
½ teaspoon freshly ground pepper

✦ **Snap** off tough ends of asparagus. Bring 2 quarts water to a boil in a Dutch oven. Add asparagus; cook 3 to 5 minutes or until crisp-tender. Rinse with cold water; drain. Cover and chill, if desired.

✦ **Melt** butter in a large skillet; add asparagus, salt, and pepper. Sauté until thoroughly heated. Serve immediately. **Yield:** 8 servings.

* Substitute 3 pounds fresh green beans for asparagus, if desired.

Spicy Green Beans with Purple Onion

(pictured on page 153)

2 pounds green beans, trimmed*
¼ cup olive oil
1 tablespoon lemon juice
1 teaspoon sugar
1 teaspoon Dijon mustard

½ teaspoon salt
¼ teaspoon pepper
2 tablespoons chopped red bell pepper
2 tablespoons sliced water chestnuts
½ cup diced purple onion

✦ **Cook** green beans in boiling salted water to cover 5 minutes or until crisp-tender; drain. Plunge into ice water to stop the cooking process; drain.
✦ **Whisk** together oil and next 5 ingredients in a large bowl. Add green beans, bell pepper, water chestnuts, and onion; toss well to coat. Cover and chill 8 hours. **Yield:** 8 servings.

* Substitute 3 (9-ounce) packages frozen whole green beans (cooked according to package directions) for fresh green beans, if desired.

Wylene B. Gillespie
Gallatin, Tennessee

A tangy marinade with a hint of lemon juice and mustard adds zest to Wylene Gillespie's homestyle green beans. Serve them with fried chicken and other comforting fare for a classic Southern supper. Turn to page 153 for a complete menu.

Broccoli Parmesan

(pictured on page 154)

1 (16-ounce) package fresh broccoli
    flowerets
2 tablespoons butter or margarine
3 tablespoons chopped onion
2 tablespoons all-purpose flour
1 teaspoon chicken bouillon granules
1¾ cups milk

½ cup freshly grated Parmesan cheese
½ teaspoon salt
½ teaspoon pepper
½ teaspoon dry mustard
¼ teaspoon ground marjoram
Grated Parmesan cheese (optional)

✦ **Arrange** broccoli in a steamer basket over boiling water. Cover and steam 5 minutes or until crisp-tender. Keep warm.
✦ **Melt** butter in a heavy saucepan; add onion, and sauté until tender. Add flour and bouillon granules, stirring until blended.
✦ **Cook,** stirring constantly, 1 minute. Gradually add milk; cook over medium heat, stirring constantly, until thickened and bubbly.
✦ **Stir** in cheese and next 4 ingredients; pour over broccoli. Sprinkle mixture with additional cheese, if desired. **Yield:** 6 servings.

Marilyn M. Fallin
Orlando, Florida

Brussels Sprouts with Parmesan Soufflés

1 pound brussels sprouts, each cut in
   half lengthwise
8 bacon slices

¼ teaspoon salt
¼ teaspoon freshly ground pepper
Parmesan Soufflés

✦ **Cook** brussels sprouts in boiling water to cover 1 minute; drain. Plunge into ice water to stop the cooking process; drain. Separate leaves; discard cores.

✦ **Cook** bacon in a large skillet until crisp; remove bacon, reserving 1 tablespoon drippings in skillet. Crumble bacon. Sauté sprout leaves, salt, and pepper in bacon drippings 1 minute. Arrange on serving plates. Top with Parmesan Soufflés; sprinkle with bacon. Serve immediately. **Yield:** 8 servings.

Parmesan Soufflés

4 frozen phyllo pastry sheets, thawed
½ cup butter, melted and divided
¼ cup all-purpose flour
⅛ teaspoon dry mustard
Pinch of ground nutmeg

1 cup milk
1 cup grated Parmesan cheese, divided
4 large eggs, separated
½ teaspoon salt
¼ teaspoon freshly ground pepper

✦ **Cut** 32 (7-inch) squares from pastry sheets. Brush squares with ¼ cup butter, and arrange into 8 stacks, staggering corners; fit stacks into 6-ounce custard cups, allowing corners to overhang edges.

✦ **Whisk** together remaining ¼ cup butter, flour, mustard, and nutmeg in a saucepan until smooth; cook over low heat, whisking constantly, 1 minute. Gradually add milk, and cook over medium heat, whisking constantly, until thickened and bubbly. Pour into a large bowl; gradually add ⅔ cup cheese. Whisk in yolks, salt, and pepper; cool to lukewarm.

✦ **Beat** egg whites until stiff peaks form; fold into cheese mixture in 2 batches. Spoon into custard cups; place in a large roasting pan. Add hot water to pan to a depth of 1 inch. Bake at 350° for 20 minutes or until slightly firm to touch; cool in water on a wire rack. Lift soufflés gently from cups; place on a greased baking sheet. Sprinkle with remaining cheese. Chill up to 4 hours, if desired.

✦ **Bake** at 375° for 10 minutes or until thoroughly heated. Serve immediately. **Yield:** 8 servings.

German-Style Red Cabbage

(pictured on page 154)

3 tablespoons butter or margarine	½ cup firmly packed brown sugar
3 Granny Smith apples, thinly sliced	2 teaspoons all-purpose flour
1 small onion, chopped	1 teaspoon salt
1 small red cabbage, shredded	¼ teaspoon pepper
⅓ cup white vinegar	⅓ cup dry red wine

✦ **Melt** butter in a skillet over medium-high heat. Add apple and onion; sauté 5 minutes. Add cabbage and vinegar.

✦ **Stir** together sugar, flour, salt, and pepper; add to skillet. Add wine. Cover, reduce heat, and simmer 35 minutes. **Yield:** 6 servings.

Kathy Wiggins
Nashville, Michigan

Dashiell Corn Pudding

(pictured on page 153)

2 (15¼-ounce) cans whole kernel corn, drained	3 tablespoons sugar
¼ cup all-purpose flour	¾ cup milk
1 tablespoon cornmeal	2 large eggs
3 tablespoons butter or margarine, melted	⅛ teaspoon ground cinnamon
	⅛ teaspoon ground nutmeg
	¼ teaspoon vanilla extract (optional)

✦ **Process** 1 can corn in an electric blender until smooth, stopping to scrape down sides. Stir together pureed corn, remaining 1 can corn, flour, and next 3 ingredients. Whisk together milk, next 3 ingredients, and, if desired, vanilla. Stir into corn mixture. Pour into a lightly greased shallow 2-quart baking dish.

✦ **Bake** at 350° for 35 minutes or until set. **Yield:** 8 servings.

Mary Kiley McMenamin
Melrose, Massachusetts

Mary Kiley McMenamin serves her Grandmother Dashiell's corn pudding during the holidays as part of a large Southern supper. Guests always ask if this sweet family favorite is dessert but are pleased to discover that it's not.

Garlic-Gruyère Mashed Potatoes

(pictured on page 150)

6 medium potatoes (4 pounds)
¾ cup hot milk
½ cup sour cream
¼ cup butter or margarine, softened
½ teaspoon salt
⅛ teaspoon ground red pepper

1 garlic clove, minced
¼ cup (1 ounce) shredded Gruyère cheese*
2 green onions, thinly sliced
⅓ cup chopped baked ham (optional)
Garnish: sliced green onions

✦ **Peel** potatoes; cut into 1-inch cubes. Cook in boiling water to cover 15 minutes or until tender. Drain.

✦ **Mash** potato with a potato masher; stir in milk and next 5 ingredients until blended. Stir in Gruyère cheese, thinly sliced green onions, and, if desired, ham. Garnish, if desired. **Yield:** 6 to 8 servings.

* Substitute ½ cup shredded Swiss cheese for Gruyère cheese, if desired.

Jeremy Bazata
Panama City, Florida

Oven-Roasted Potatoes, Green Beans, and Onions

(pictured on page 150)

¼ cup olive oil
1 garlic clove, crushed
½ teaspoon salt
½ teaspoon freshly ground black pepper

3 medium onions, quartered
2 pounds small round red potatoes, cut into ¼-inch-thick slices
1½ pounds fresh green beans, untrimmed

✦ **Stir** together first 4 ingredients; set aside 1 tablespoon oil mixture. Place onion wedges and potato slices in a greased roasting pan, and drizzle with remaining oil mixture, stirring gently.

✦ **Roast** at 450° on bottom rack of oven 25 minutes, stirring occasionally.

✦ **Add** green beans to pan; drizzle reserved 1 tablespoon oil mixture over beans, stirring gently. Roast 15 to 20 more minutes or until vegetables are tender, stirring occasionally. **Yield:** 8 servings.

Sweet Potato-Eggnog Casserole

5 pounds large sweet
   potatoes
½ cup golden raisins
¼ cup brandy
⅔ cup refrigerated eggnog

3 tablespoons butter or margarine,
   melted
2 tablespoons sugar
⅛ teaspoon salt
Oatmeal Cookie Topping

✦ **Cook** sweet potatoes in water to cover in a large Dutch oven 40 minutes or until tender; drain and cool to touch. Peel and mash.

✦ **Combine** raisins and brandy; let stand 30 minutes. Drain. Combine potato, eggnog, and next 3 ingredients; reserve 2 cups. Stir raisins into remaining potato mixture; spoon into a lightly greased 2-quart baking dish. Sprinkle with Oatmeal Cookie Topping. Pipe or dollop reserved potato mixture around edge of casserole. Bake at 350° for 20 minutes or until heated. **Yield:** 6 to 8 servings.

Oatmeal Cookie Topping

2 (2-inch) oatmeal cookies, crumbled
2 tablespoons dark brown sugar

2 tablespoons chopped pecans,
   toasted

✦ **Combine** ingredients in a small bowl. **Yield:** ½ cup.

Mary G. Swift
New Orleans, Louisiana

> *"I like to be creative in the kitchen—open the refrigerator door and improvise with what's there. One Thanksgiving, I found a little eggnog on the shelf and added it to my sweet potatoes. I've been making the potatoes that way ever since."*
> *—Mary G. Swift*

Roasted Winter Vegetables

(pictured on pages 84 and 151)

4 parsnips, peeled
4 turnips, peeled
½ medium rutabaga, peeled
½ medium butternut squash, peeled
2 quarts water

2 tablespoons kosher salt, divided
¼ cup all-purpose flour
1 teaspoon freshly ground pepper
⅓ cup butter or margarine, melted

✦ **Cut** parsnips into 1-inch slices; cut turnips, rutabaga, and squash into 1-inch cubes. Bring parsnip, turnip, rutabaga, 2 quarts water, and 1 tablespoon salt to a boil in a Dutch oven; boil, stirring occasionally, 5 minutes.

✦ **Add** squash; cook 7 to 10 minutes or until squash is slightly tender. Drain vegetables, and cool. Cover and chill up to 8 hours, if desired.

✦ **Combine** remaining salt, flour, and pepper in a heavy-duty, zip-top plastic bag; add one-third of vegetables. Seal; shake until coated. Place vegetables in a single layer in a large greased roasting pan. Repeat procedure with remaining vegetables and flour mixture. Drizzle vegetables with butter, tossing gently.

✦ **Bake** at 375° for 30 minutes or until golden. Serve immediately. **Yield:** 8 servings.

Chunky Applesauce

6 large Granny Smith or other cooking apples, peeled and sliced
1 cup water

½ teaspoon ground cinnamon
¼ teaspoon ground nutmeg
¼ cup firmly packed brown sugar

✦ **Combine** apple slices and 1 cup water in a Dutch oven; bring to a boil. Cover, reduce heat, and simmer 40 minutes, stirring occasionally.

✦ **Add** cinnamon and nutmeg; cook, uncovered, over medium heat 10 minutes or until liquid is evaporated. Remove from heat; stir in brown sugar. Cool at least 30 minutes. **Yield:** 8 servings.

Brandied Cranberry Oranges

Blood oranges make their appearance in the midst of the holiday season. The juicy, burgundy-colored fruit has rich citrus flavor with a hint of raspberry.

6 fresh blood red oranges or navel oranges
2 (12-ounce) packages fresh or frozen cranberries, thawed

3 cups sugar
1 cup orange juice
½ cup plus 2 tablespoons brandy (optional)

✦ **Peel** oranges, if desired. Cut oranges into ⅛-inch slices, discarding ends. Cut slices into quarters.

✦ **Layer** one-third of orange slices, one-third of cranberries, and 1 cup sugar in a large bowl. Repeat layers twice with remaining fruit and sugar. Cover and let stand 8 hours.

✦ **Spoon** mixture into a Dutch oven. Stir in orange juice; bring to a boil, and boil, stirring constantly, until sugar dissolves.

✦ **Pack** hot fruit into jars, filling to ½ inch from top. Add 2 tablespoons brandy to each jar, if desired. Cover fruit with boiling syrup, filling to ½ inch from top. Remove air bubbles; wipe jar rims. Cover at once with metal lids; screw on bands. Process in a boiling-water bath 15 minutes. **Yield:** 5 pints.

Mrs. Donald MacMillan
Cartersville, Georgia

Congealed Cherry Salad

1 (16-ounce) can pitted dark sweet
   cherries, undrained
1 (11-ounce) can mandarin oranges,
   undrained
1 (8-ounce) can crushed pineapple,
   undrained

1 (6-ounce) package cherry-flavored
   gelatin
1 cup cold water
½ cup chopped pecans
Lettuce leaves

✦ **Drain** all canned fruit into a bowl, reserving juice. Set fruit aside. Stir juice well, and reserve 1½ cups juice. Bring reserved juice to a boil in a saucepan. Add gelatin; cook, stirring constantly, 2 minutes or until gelatin dissolves. Remove from heat. Stir in cold water. Chill until the consistency of unbeaten egg white.

✦ **Fold** in drained fruit and pecans. Pour into a lightly oiled 6-cup mold. Cover and chill until firm. Unmold onto a lettuce-lined serving plate. **Yield:** 8 to 10 servings.

Note: To unmold with ease, run a knife around edge of mold to break the suction. Gently pull salad away from sides of mold using fingers. Wrap mold in a damp, warm cloth towel. Place a serving platter on top of mold, and invert. Remove mold.

Waldorf Rice Salad

2 oranges, peeled, sectioned, and
   chopped
1 Red Delicious apple, unpeeled and
   chopped
1 ripe pear, unpeeled and chopped
2 cups cooked long-grain brown and
   wild rice blend (we tested with
   Uncle Ben's)

½ cup chopped celery
⅓ cup dried sweetened cranberries
   (we tested with Ocean Spray
   Craisins)
½ cup mayonnaise
¼ cup sour cream
Red leaf lettuce leaves
½ cup chopped walnuts, toasted

✦ **Combine** first 6 ingredients in a large bowl.
✦ **Stir** together mayonnaise and sour cream; add to fruit mixture, tossing well. Cover and chill.
✦ **Spoon** salad mixture onto individual lettuce-lined salad plates. Sprinkle with walnuts just before serving. **Yield:** 8 servings.

Winter Green Holiday Salad With Cranberry Vinaigrette

¾ cup pecan halves
⅔ cup honey
¼ cup butter or margarine, melted
½ cup sugar
4 heads Belgian endive
2 large watercress bunches
8 kumquats

4 cups finely shredded radicchio
3 seedless tangerines, peeled and sectioned
Cranberry Vinaigrette (see facing page)
1 cup fresh mint leaves, shredded
Garnish: fresh mint sprigs

✦ **Stir** together first 3 ingredients; spread evenly in a shallow roasting pan.
✦ **Bake** at 325° for 12 to 15 minutes, stirring often. Remove pecans with a slotted spoon; toss pecans with sugar. Cool.
✦ **Separate** endive leaves; cut larger leaves in half. Discard coarse watercress stems. Cut kumquats in half lengthwise.
✦ **Toss** together endive, watercress, kumquats, radicchio, and next 3 ingredients. Sprinkle with pecans. Garnish, if desired. **Yield:** 8 servings.

Cranberry Vinaigrette

½ cup fresh cranberries
⅔ cup tangerine juice
⅓ cup tarragon vinegar
2 tablespoons Dijon mustard

2 shallots, minced
½ teaspoon salt
½ teaspoon pepper
½ cup walnut oil or light olive oil

✦ **Bring** cranberries and tangerine juice to a boil in a medium saucepan over medium-high heat; boil 5 minutes. Drain, reserving juice. Set cranberries aside. Return juice to pan, and boil 5 minutes.

✦ **Process** juice, vinegar, and next 4 ingredients in a blender until blended. With blender running, add oil in a slow, steady stream. Stir in cranberries. **Yield:** 1½ cups.

Susan Asanovic
Wilton, Connecticut

Spinach Salad with Feta Cheese and Basil Dressing

½ cup olive oil
¼ cup red wine vinegar
2 teaspoons sugar
¼ teaspoon salt
¼ teaspoon pepper
5 fresh basil leaves, chopped
1 garlic clove, minced

1 pound fresh spinach
1 ripe avocado, peeled and sliced
½ cup crumbled feta cheese
½ cup pine nuts or chopped walnuts, toasted
Kalamata olives (optional)

✦ **Combine** first 7 ingredients in a jar. Cover tightly, and shake vigorously. Chill dressing 2 hours.

✦ **Remove** stems from spinach; wash leaves thoroughly, and pat dry. Tear leaves into bite-size pieces.

✦ **Combine** spinach, avocado, feta cheese, pine nuts, and, if desired, olives, in a large bowl; toss gently. Pour dressing over salad, and toss gently. Serve immediately. **Yield:** 10 servings.

Best Barbecue Coleslaw

Serve this zesty slaw with leftover turkey sandwiches
for a flavorful day-after-Christmas lunch.

2 (10-ounce) packages finely shredded
  cabbage
1 carrot, shredded
½ cup sugar
½ cup mayonnaise
¼ cup milk

¼ cup buttermilk
2½ tablespoons lemon juice
1½ tablespoons white vinegar
½ teaspoon salt
⅛ teaspoon pepper

✦ **Combine** cabbage and carrot in a large bowl.

✦ **Whisk** together sugar and remaining 7 ingredients until blended; toss with vegetables. Cover and chill at least 2 hours. **Yield:** 8 to 10 servings.

Robert Peacock
Birmingham, Alabama

Black-Eyed Pea Salad

4 celery ribs, chopped
1 small green or red bell pepper,
  chopped
4 green onions, chopped
2 (15.5-ounce) cans black-eyed peas,
  rinsed and drained

⅓ cup minced fresh cilantro or parsley
⅓ cup Italian dressing
2 tablespoons country-style Dijon
  mustard
Leaf lettuce (optional)

✦ **Combine** first 7 ingredients in a large bowl. Cover and chill at least 4 hours. Serve over lettuce, if desired. **Yield:** 6 servings.

Spicy Potato Salad

4 large round red potatoes (about
  2 pounds)
⅓ cup vegetable oil
¼ cup white vinegar
1 tablespoon sugar
1½ teaspoons chili powder
1 teaspoon seasoned salt

⅛ teaspoon hot sauce
1 (8¾-ounce) can whole kernel corn,
  drained
1 small carrot, shredded
1 (2.5-ounce) can sliced ripe olives,
  drained
4 green onions, sliced

✦ **Cook** potatoes in boiling water to cover 20 to 30 minutes or until tender. Drain and cool to touch. Cut potatoes into cubes; place in a large bowl.

✦ **Whisk** together oil and next 5 ingredients; pour over potato, tossing gently. Chill 1 hour. Stir in corn and remaining ingredients. **Yield:** 8 to 10 servings.

Dawn's World-Famous Greek Salad

1 pound unpeeled jumbo fresh shrimp
1 quart boiling water
1 head romaine lettuce
Greek Potato Salad
1 head iceberg lettuce, shredded
14 pickled beets, sliced
1 cucumber, peeled and cut into strips
2 ripe tomatoes, cut into wedges
  (optional)

½ cup pitted kalamata olives
1 (8-ounce) package feta cheese,
  crumbled
3 green bell pepper slices
1 (2-ounce) can anchovies (optional)
1 teaspoon chopped fresh oregano
½ cup red wine vinegar
½ cup olive oil

✦ **Cook** shrimp in 1 quart boiling water 3 to 5 minutes or just until shrimp turn pink; drain. Rinse with cold water. Peel shrimp, leaving tails on; devein, if desired.

✦ **Line** a large platter with romaine lettuce leaves. Mound Greek Potato Salad in center. Arrange shrimp, iceberg lettuce, beets, cucumber, and, if desired, tomato around potato salad.

✦ **Sprinkle** with olives and feta cheese. Top with bell pepper slices, and, if desired, anchovies; sprinkle with oregano. Drizzle with vinegar and oil just before serving. **Yield:** 6 to 8 servings.

Greek Potato Salad

2 pounds new potatoes
¼ cup olive oil
¼ cup red wine vinegar
3 tablespoons mayonnaise

½ teaspoon salt
½ teaspoon pepper
½ teaspoon dried oregano

✦ **Cook** potatoes in boiling salted water to cover 30 minutes. Cool slightly. Cut into 1-inch pieces.

✦ **Whisk** together oil and remaining 5 ingredients; toss mixture with potato. **Yield:** 5 cups.

Dawn Sumner Titmas
Mill Creek, Washington

Dawn Sumner Titmas has warm memories of growing up in St. Petersburg, Florida, a region that helped shape her culinary preferences. She and her husband now live in Washington, and when she misses the Southern and Cuban ingredients for her favorite recipes, she turns to her family for help. She says, "My mother visits with her suitcases bulging with grits, Vigo yellow rice, dried black beans, and chorizo!"

Dawn prefers that salads have a home-made dressing and fresh tomatoes. Her flavorful salad is a meal in itself.

Classic Holiday Desserts

Delight guests of all ages with this splendid selection of classic holiday desserts. ✦ Impress your guests with deceptively simple Red Velvet Peppermint Cake (page 108). It provides all the scrumptious flavor of the ruby-colored original but offers the convenience of today's timesaving cake mixes. ✦ Tempt a cheesecake-lover with Coconut-Chocolate-Almond Cheesecake (page 112), a rich dessert that will bring to mind a famous coconut candy bar. ✦ Create a new family favorite with Applesauce Pie (page 115). It begins with an easy home-made applesauce and ends with second helpings.

Coconut-Chocolate-Almond Cheesecake, page 112

Best Carrot Cake

Buttermilk Glaze adds moisture to this carrot cake, while swirls of frosting provide a classic finishing touch.

2 cups all-purpose flour
2 teaspoons baking soda
½ teaspoon salt
2 teaspoons ground cinnamon
3 large eggs
2 cups sugar
¾ cup vegetable oil
¾ cup buttermilk

2 teaspoons vanilla extract
2 cups grated carrot
1 (8-ounce) can crushed pineapple, drained
1 (3½-ounce) can flaked coconut
1 cup chopped pecans or walnuts
Buttermilk Glaze
Cream Cheese Frosting

✦ **Line** 3 (9-inch) round cakepans with wax paper; lightly grease and flour wax paper. Set pans aside.

✦ **Stir** together first 4 ingredients. Beat eggs and next 4 ingredients at medium speed with an electric mixer until smooth. Add flour mixture, beating at low speed until blended. Fold in carrot and next 3 ingredients. Pour batter into prepared cakepans.

✦ **Bake** at 350° for 25 to 30 minutes or until a wooden pick inserted in center comes out clean.

✦ **Drizzle** Buttermilk Glaze evenly over layers; cool layers in pans on wire racks 15 minutes. Remove from pans; cool completely on wire racks.

✦ **Spread** Cream Cheese Frosting between layers and on top and sides of cake. **Yield:** 1 (3-layer) cake.

Buttermilk Glaze

1 cup sugar
1½ teaspoons baking soda
½ cup buttermilk

½ cup butter or margarine
1 tablespoon light corn syrup
1 teaspoon vanilla extract

✦ **Bring** first 5 ingredients to a boil in a large Dutch oven over medium-high heat. Boil, stirring often, 4 minutes. Remove from heat, and stir in vanilla. **Yield:** 1½ cups.

Cream Cheese Frosting

1 (8-ounce) package cream cheese, softened
1 (3-ounce) package cream cheese, softened

¾ cup butter or margarine, softened
1 (16-ounce) package powdered sugar, sifted
1½ teaspoons vanilla extract

✦ **Beat** first 3 ingredients at medium speed with an electric mixer until creamy. Add powdered sugar and vanilla; beat until smooth. **Yield:** 4 cups.

Phyllis Vanhoy
Salisbury, North Carolina

Italian Cream Cake

(pictured on cover)

This cake is sure to win raves from your family—it did in our Test Kitchens.

½ cup butter or margarine, softened
½ cup shortening
2 cups sugar
5 large eggs, separated
1 tablespoon vanilla extract
2 cups all-purpose flour

1 teaspoon baking soda
1 cup buttermilk
1 cup flaked coconut
Nutty Cream Cheese Frosting
Garnishes: toasted pecan halves,
    chopped pecans

✦ **Beat** butter and shortening in a large mixing bowl at medium speed with an electric mixer until creamy; gradually add sugar, beating well. Add egg yolks, one at a time, beating until blended after each addition. Add vanilla; beat until blended.

✦ **Combine** flour and soda; add to butter mixture alternately with buttermilk, beginning and ending with flour mixture. Beat at low speed until blended after each addition. Stir in coconut.

✦ **Beat** egg whites until stiff peaks form; fold into batter. Pour into 3 greased and floured 9-inch round cakepans.

✦ **Bake** at 350° for 25 minutes or until a wooden pick inserted in center comes out clean. Cool layers in pans on wire racks 10 minutes; remove from pans, and cool completely on wire racks.

✦ **Spread** Nutty Cream Cheese Frosting between layers and on top and sides of cake. Garnish, if desired. **Yield:** 1 (3-layer) cake.

Nutty Cream Cheese Frosting

1 cup chopped pecans
1 (8-ounce) package cream cheese,
    softened
½ cup butter or margarine, softened

1 tablespoon vanilla extract
1 (16-ounce) package powdered
    sugar, sifted

✦ **Bake** pecans in a shallow pan at 350°, stirring occasionally, 5 to 10 minutes or until toasted. Cool.

✦ **Beat** cream cheese, butter, and vanilla at medium speed with an electric mixer until creamy. Add sugar, beating at low speed until blended. Beat at high speed until smooth; stir in pecans. **Yield:** about 4 cups.

Donna Willcut
Pryor, Oklahoma

Red Velvet Peppermint Cake

The cake batter is swirled right in the pans. Landscaping this confection is a project your whole family can enjoy.

1 (18.25-ounce) package white cake mix (we tested with Duncan Hines)
3 egg whites
1⅓ cups buttermilk
2 tablespoons vegetable oil
1 (9-ounce) package yellow cake mix (we tested with Jiffy)*
½ cup buttermilk
1 large egg
1½ tablespoons cocoa
½ teaspoon baking soda
2 tablespoons liquid red food coloring (we tested with McCormick)
1 teaspoon cider vinegar
Peppermint Cream Cheese Frosting
Garnishes: Holiday Trees; 6 (5-inch) red-and-white peppermint candy canes, crushed; 12 (5-inch) green candy canes, broken; 12 round peppermint candies

✦ **Beat** first 4 ingredients according to white cake mix package directions.
Beat yellow cake mix and next 6 ingredients according to package directions.

Spoon red batter alternately with white batter evenly into 3 greased and floured 9-inch round cakepans. Swirl batter gently with a knife.

✦ **Bake** at 350° for 22 to 25 minutes or until a wooden pick inserted in center comes out clean. Cool layers in pans on wire racks 10 minutes. Remove from pans, and cool completely on wire racks.

✦ **Spread** Peppermint Cream Cheese Frosting between layers and on top and sides of cake. (If desired, chill cake up to 2 days, or freeze up to 1 month. If you freeze cake, thaw it completely before garnishing to prevent the crushed candy from running. Do not refrigerate or freeze after garnishing.) Garnish, if desired; serve within 2 hours of garnishing. **Yield:** 1 (3-layer) cake.

* Substitute 1¾ cups yellow cake mix from another brand's larger box, if desired.

Peppermint Cream Cheese Frosting

1 (8-ounce) package cream cheese, softened
1 cup butter or margarine, softened
1 (32-ounce) package powdered sugar
2 teaspoons peppermint extract or vanilla extract

✦ **Beat** cream cheese and butter at medium speed with an electric mixer until creamy. Gradually add sugar, beating at low speed until smooth. Add peppermint extract, beating until blended. **Yield:** about 5 cups.

Quick Peppermint Frosting option: Stir together 3 (16-ounce) containers ready-to-spread cream cheese frosting and 2 teaspoons peppermint extract.

Holiday Trees

1 (16-ounce) package powdered sugar
3 tablespoons meringue powder
6 to 8 tablespoons warm water
6 (4-inch) sugar ice-cream cones
12 (5-inch) red-and-white candy canes, coarsely crushed
12 (5-inch) green candy canes, coarsely crushed
Edible glitter or sparkling sugar (optional)

✦ **Beat** first 3 ingredients at low speed with an electric mixer until blended. Beat at high speed 4 to 5 minutes or until stiff peaks form. If icing is too stiff, add additional water, ¼ teaspoon at a time, until desired consistency.

✦ **Spoon** icing into a heavy-duty, zip-top plastic bag; seal. Snip a ¼-inch hole in 1 corner of bag. Pipe 2 rows of points around 1 cone, beginning at large end and working upward, to resemble a tree. Sprinkle with crushed candy and, if desired, glitter. Repeat procedure until cone is decorated.

✦ **Invert** 2 cones, and stack together, securing with a small amount of icing; repeat decorating procedure. Invert remaining 3 cones, and stack together, securing with icing; repeat decorating procedure. Insert larger candy pieces into trees, if desired. Let stand 8 hours. Store in a cool, dry place up to 1 month. **Yield:** 3 trees.

Chocolate Truffle Cake

You can freeze the cake layers several weeks ahead;
then assemble the cake a day or two before your holiday party.

1 cup butter, softened
1¼ cups sugar
3 large eggs
2 cups sifted cake flour
1 teaspoon baking soda
¼ teaspoon salt
⅓ cup cocoa
1 (8-ounce) container sour cream

2 teaspoons vanilla extract
1 recipe Chocolate-Praline Truffles (see recipe on page 136; omit pecan mixture)
White Chocolate-Buttercream Frosting
1 (4-ounce) white chocolate bar, shaved

✦ **Beat** butter at medium speed with an electric mixer until creamy; gradually add sugar, beating well. Add eggs, one at a time, beating until blended after each addition. Combine flour and next 3 ingredients; add to butter mixture alternately with sour cream, beginning and ending with flour mixture. Beat at low speed until blended after each addition. Stir in vanilla. Pour batter into 3 greased and floured 8-inch round cakepans.

✦ **Bake** at 350° for 18 to 20 minutes or until a wooden pick inserted in center comes out clean. Cool layers in pans on wire racks 10 minutes. Remove from pans; cool completely on wire racks.

✦ **Prepare** mixture for Chocolate-Praline Truffles; spread a thin layer between cake layers and on top and sides of cake. (If any truffle mixture remains, cover

and chill until firm enough to shape into balls; then shape into balls, and roll in powdered sugar or cocoa.) Cover and chill cake at least 1 hour.

✦ **Spoon** ½ cup White Chocolate-Buttercream Frosting into a heavy-duty, zip-top plastic bag; seal bag, and set aside in refrigerator. Spread remaining frosting on top and sides of cake. Remove reserved frosting from refrigerator; snip a ¼-inch hole in 1 corner of bag. Pipe frosting around base of cake, creating a small ruffle. Sprinkle shaved white chocolate on top of cake. Chill at least 1 hour and up to 2 days. **Yield:** 1 (3-layer) cake.

White Chocolate-Buttercream Frosting

3 ounces white chocolate, broken into pieces	4½ cups sifted powdered sugar
¼ cup whipping cream, divided	1½ teaspoons vanilla extract
¾ cup butter, softened	

✦ **Microwave** chocolate and 2 tablespoons whipping cream in a 1-quart microwave-safe bowl at MEDIUM (50% power) 45 seconds. Whisk until chocolate melts and mixture is smooth. (Do not overheat.)

✦ **Beat** butter and ¾ cup sugar at low speed with an electric mixer until blended. Add remaining sugar alternately with remaining 2 tablespoons whipping cream; beat at low speed until blended after each addition.

✦ **Add** chocolate mixture and vanilla. Beat at medium speed until spreading consistency. **Yield:** 3 cups.

Cream Cheese Pound Cake

Our Test Kitchens staff gave this cake the highest mark a recipe can get.

1½ cups butter, softened	6 large eggs
1 (8-ounce) package cream cheese, softened	1½ teaspoons vanilla extract
3 cups sugar	3 cups all-purpose flour
	⅛ teaspoon salt

✦ **Beat** butter and cream cheese at medium speed with an electric mixer 2 minutes or until mixture is creamy. Gradually add sugar, beating 5 to 7 minutes. Add eggs, one at a time, beating just until yellow disappears. Add vanilla, mixing well. Combine flour and salt; gradually add to butter mixture, beating at low speed just until blended after each addition. Pour batter into a greased and floured 10-inch tube pan. Fill a 2-cup, ovenproof measuring cup with water, and place in oven with tube pan.

✦ **Bake** at 300° for 1 hour and 45 minutes or until a wooden pick inserted in center of cake comes out clean. Cool in pan on a wire rack 10 to 15 minutes; remove from pan, and cool completely on wire rack. **Yield:** 1 (10-inch) cake.

Eddy McGee
Elkin, North Carolina

Coconut-Chocolate-Almond Cheesecake

(pictured on page 104)

This rich, decadent dessert is the perfect finale to an elegant Christmas dinner. Sprinkle chopped almonds around the outer edge of the cheesecake for a simple, yet showy, garnish.

Darlene Evans is known as the "Cheesecake Lady" among her colleagues at a Birmingham law firm. She dreamed up this fabulous cheese-cake while standing in line at a grocery store.

She remembers, "I saw the ingredients on the shelves and thought, 'What a great combination that would be.'"

1½ cups chocolate wafer cookie crumbs (28 to 30 cookies) (we tested with Nabisco)
3 tablespoons sugar
¼ cup butter or margarine, melted
4 (8-ounce) packages cream cheese, softened
3 large eggs
1 cup sugar
1 (14-ounce) package flaked coconut
1 (11.5-ounce) package milk chocolate morsels
½ cup slivered almonds, toasted
1 teaspoon vanilla extract
½ cup (3 ounces) semisweet chocolate morsels
Garnish: toasted chopped almonds

✦ **Stir** together first 3 ingredients; press mixture into bottom of a 10-inch springform pan. Bake at 350° for 8 minutes. Cool.

✦ **Beat** cream cheese, eggs, and 1 cup sugar at medium speed with an electric mixer until fluffy.

✦ **Stir** in coconut and next 3 ingredients. Pour batter into prepared crust.

✦ **Bake** at 350° for 1 hour. Cool on a wire rack.

✦ **Place** semisweet chocolate morsels in a heavy-duty, zip-top plastic bag; seal. Submerge bag in warm water until morsels melt. Snip a tiny hole in 1 corner of bag; drizzle chocolate over cheesecake.

✦ **Cover** cheesecake, and chill at least 8 hours. Store in refrigerator up to 5 days, if desired. Remove sides of springform pan when ready to serve. Garnish cheesecake, if desired. **Yield:** 12 servings.

Darlene Evans
Birmingham, Alabama

Ultimate Cheesecake

2 cups graham cracker crumbs
¼ cup sugar
½ cup butter or margarine, melted
7 large eggs
4 (8-ounce) packages cream cheese, softened
1¾ cups sugar

2 teaspoons vanilla extract
1 (16-ounce) container sour cream
½ cup sugar
⅛ teaspoon vanilla extract
Apricot Glaze
Garnish: strawberry halves

✦ **Stir** together first 3 ingredients; press into bottom and 1 inch up sides of a 10-inch springform pan. Chill 1 hour.

✦ **Beat** eggs at medium speed with an electric mixer. Add cream cheese; beat until blended. Gradually add 1¾ cups sugar, beating well.

✦ **Stir** in 2 teaspoons vanilla. Pour batter into chilled crust.

✦ **Bake** at 350° for 1 hour and 15 minutes. Cool on a wire rack 10 minutes. Increase oven temperature to 425°.

✦ **Stir** together sour cream, ½ cup sugar, and ⅛ teaspoon vanilla; spread over cheesecake.

✦ **Bake** at 425° for 5 to 7 minutes. Cool on a wire rack 1 hour. Cover and chill at least 10 hours. Remove sides of springform pan when ready to serve. Serve cheesecake with Apricot Glaze. Garnish, if desired. **Yield:** 12 servings.

Apricot Glaze

1 (10-ounce) jar apricot jam
¼ cup sugar

¼ cup water
1 tablespoon rum or brandy

✦ **Stir** together first 3 ingredients in a small saucepan; cook over low heat, stirring occasionally, until consistency of syrup. Remove from heat.

✦ **Stir** in rum; pour through a fine wire-mesh strainer into a bowl. Cool; serve over cheesecake slices. **Yield:** 1½ cups.

Cherry Glaze: Substitute cherry preserves for apricot jam; do not strain before serving.

Diana Hill
Arcadia, Florida

Pear-Mincemeat Pie

3 pounds pears, peeled and diced
1 (15-ounce) package raisins
3½ cups sugar
⅓ cup cider vinegar
½ teaspoon salt
1½ teaspoons ground nutmeg
1½ teaspoons ground cinnamon

1½ teaspoons ground allspice
1½ teaspoons ground cloves
1 (15-ounce) package refrigerated
      piecrusts
½ cup chopped pecans, toasted
1 large egg, lightly beaten

✦ **Bring** first 9 ingredients to a boil in a large heavy saucepan, stirring often;
reduce heat to medium-high, and cook, stirring often, 25 to 30 minutes or until
thickened. Cool.

✦ **Fit** 1 piecrust into a 9-inch deep-dish pieplate according to package directions. Stir pecans into pear mixture; spoon into prepared piecrust.

✦ **Roll** remaining piecrust to press out fold lines. Cut out leaf shapes from
center of piecrust, using a leaf-shaped cookie cutter and leaving a 3-inch
border around edges.

✦ **Place** piecrust carefully over filling, and fold edges under. Make diagonal
cuts into edge at ¼-inch intervals, and fold every other piece inward. Brush
piecrust and leaves with egg. Arrange leaves on pie.

✦ **Bake** on lowest oven rack at 350° for 1 hour or until golden, shielding with
aluminum foil to prevent excessive browning, if necessary. **Yield:** 1 (9-inch) pie.

Barbara McCool
Gore Springs, Mississippi

Applesauce Pie

10 large Granny Smith apples, peeled
    and chopped
1 large lemon, sliced and seeded
2½ cups sugar
3 tablespoons butter or margarine

1 teaspoon vanilla extract
1 (15-ounce) package refrigerated
    piecrusts
Spiced Ice Cream

✦ **Cook** first 3 ingredients in a Dutch oven over medium heat, stirring often, 35 minutes or until thickened. Remove from heat. Discard lemon. Add butter and vanilla. Cool.

✦ **Fit** 1 piecrust into a 9-inch pieplate according to package directions. Pour applesauce mixture into crust.

✦ **Roll** remaining piecrust to press out fold lines; cut into ½-inch strips. Reserve 4 strips.

✦ **Arrange** remaining strips in a lattice design over filling; fold edges under, and crimp.

✦ **Cut** reserved pastry strips in half lengthwise. Lay halves side by side, and twist; arrange around inner edge of pie.

✦ **Bake** on lowest oven rack at 425° for 30 to 35 minutes or until golden, shielding with aluminum foil to prevent excessive browning, if necessary. Serve with Spiced Ice Cream. **Yield:** 1 (9-inch) pie.

Spiced Ice Cream

1 quart vanilla ice cream, softened
1 teaspoon ground cinnamon

½ teaspoon ground nutmeg

✦ **Stir** together all ingredients. Freeze. **Yield:** 1 quart.

Aunt Kitty's Lemon Pie

1 unbaked 9-inch pastry shell
1½ cups sugar
⅓ cup butter or margarine, softened
3 large eggs

1 tablespoon grated lemon rind
¼ cup fresh lemon juice
¼ teaspoon salt
½ teaspoon lemon extract

✦ **Line** pastry shell with aluminum foil; fill with pie weights or dried beans.

✦ **Bake** at 425° for 7 minutes; remove weights and foil.

✦ **Whisk** together sugar and butter until blended. Whisk in eggs and remaining 4 ingredients. Pour into piecrust.

✦ **Bake** at 350° for 30 minutes or until set. Cool pie on a wire rack. **Yield:** 1 (9-inch) pie.

Mary Kiley McMenamin
Melrose, Massachusetts

This tart lemon pie from Mary Kiley McMenamin's aunt is the perfect ending to a comforting meal of fried chicken, corn pudding, and other Southern favorites. Turn to page 153 for the rest of the menu.

Mom's Pecan Pie

½ (15-ounce) package refrigerated
   piecrusts
4 large eggs
1 cup dark corn syrup
¾ cup sugar

⅓ cup butter or margarine, melted
Pinch of salt
1 teaspoon vanilla extract
1 cup chopped pecans
¾ cup pecan halves

✦ **Fit** piecrust into a 9-inch pieplate according to package directions; fold edges under, and crimp.

✦ **Beat** eggs and next 5 ingredients at medium speed with an electric mixer until smooth. Stir in chopped pecans; pour into crust. Arrange pecan halves on top of pie.

✦ **Bake** at 350° for 50 minutes, shielding edges with aluminum foil after 30 minutes to prevent excessive browning. **Yield:** 1 (9-inch) pie.

Mary Lou Edwards
Mesa, Arizona

Bourbon-Chocolate Pecan Pie

½ (15-ounce) package refrigerated
   piecrusts
4 large eggs
1 cup light corn syrup
6 tablespoons butter or margarine,
   melted
½ cup sugar

¼ cup firmly packed light brown sugar
3 tablespoons bourbon
1 tablespoon all-purpose flour
1 tablespoon vanilla extract
1 cup coarsely chopped pecans
1 cup (6 ounces) semisweet chocolate
   morsels

✦ **Fit** piecrust into a 9-inch pieplate according to package directions; fold edges under, and crimp.

◆ **Whisk** together eggs and next 7 ingredients until mixture is smooth; stir in pecans and morsels. Pour into piecrust.

◆ **Bake** pie on lowest oven rack at 350° for 1 hour or until filling is set. **Yield:** 1 (9-inch) pie.

Chocolate Heaven

1 cup walnuts
1 cup all-purpose flour
½ cup firmly packed light brown sugar
6 tablespoons butter or margarine, melted
1 (8-ounce) package cream cheese, softened

⅔ cup butter or margarine, softened
1⅔ cups powdered sugar
8 (1-ounce) semisweet chocolate squares, melted
¼ cup Irish cream liqueur
½ pint whipping cream
1 tablespoon powdered sugar

◆ **Process** first 3 ingredients in a food processor until walnuts are ground, stopping to scrape down sides. Add melted butter; process until blended. Press mixture into bottom and up sides of a 9-inch pieplate.

◆ **Bake** at 350° for 12 to 15 minutes or until lightly browned. Cool.

◆ **Beat** cream cheese and ⅔ cup butter at medium speed with an electric mixer until smooth; add 1⅔ cups powdered sugar, beating until blended. Add chocolate and liqueur, beating until blended. Spoon into prepared crust, and chill 8 hours. Store in refrigerator up to 4 days, if desired.

◆ **Beat** whipping cream at medium speed until foamy; add 1 tablespoon powdered sugar, beating until stiff peaks form. Spread on top of pie just before serving. **Yield:** 1 (9-inch) pie.

Andrea Schackor Lerbs
League City, Texas

Brownie-Mint Pie

1 (4.6-ounce) package chocolate mints (we tested with Andes)
1 (15.8-ounce) package brownie mix

1 unbaked 9-inch deep-dish frozen pastry shell
Vanilla ice cream
Hot fudge topping

◆ **Chop** chocolate mints, and set aside 3 tablespoons. Prepare brownie mix according to package directions, stirring remaining chopped mints into brownie batter. Pour into pastry shell.

◆ **Bake** at 350° for 45 minutes or until done; cool slightly. Serve with ice cream, hot fudge topping, and reserved 3 tablespoons chopped mints. **Yield:** 1 (9-inch) pie.

Double-Chocolate Bombe

*This bombe is easy to make, even though it has a lot of steps.
And the oohs and aahs that will fill the room when you serve
it will make it worth the time it took to prepare.*

½ cup pecan pieces, toasted
¼ cup butter, softened
¼ cup shortening
1 cup sugar
1½ teaspoons vanilla extract
3 large eggs, separated
1 cup all-purpose flour

½ teaspoon baking soda
½ cup buttermilk
Chocolate Mousse
White Chocolate Mousse
Chocolate Ganache
Garnish: chocolate curls

✦ **Process** pecans in a food processor until ground; set aside.

✦ **Beat** butter and shortening at medium speed with an electric mixer until creamy; gradually add sugar, beating well. Add vanilla, beating until blended. Add egg yolks, one at a time, beating until blended after each addition.

✦ **Combine** flour, soda, and ground pecans; add to creamed mixture alternately with buttermilk, beginning and ending with flour mixture. Beat at low speed until blended after each addition.

✦ **Beat** egg whites until stiff peaks form; fold into batter. Pour mixture into a well-greased and floured 15- x 10-inch jellyroll pan.

✦ **Bake** at 350° for 20 minutes or until a wooden pick inserted in center comes out clean. Cool in pan on a wire rack 10 minutes; remove from pan, and cool completely on wire rack.

✦ **Line** a 3-quart mixing bowl (8½ inches across) with plastic wrap. Cut cake lengthwise into 2-inch strips; line prepared bowl with cake strips, reserving remaining strips. Spread Chocolate Mousse over cake in bowl; cover and chill 1 hour.

✦ **Pour** White Chocolate Mousse into bowl over chocolate layer. Cover and chill 1 more hour. Cover with remaining cake strips. Cover and chill at least 8 hours.

✦ **Invert** bombe onto a large cake plate; spread Chocolate Ganache over bombe. Garnish, if desired. **Yield:** 8 to 10 servings.

Chocolate Mousse

1 cup whipping cream, divided
1 (8-ounce) package semisweet
    chocolate squares
¼ cup light corn syrup

¼ cup butter
2 tablespoons powdered sugar
½ teaspoon vanilla extract

✦ **Cook** ¼ cup whipping cream and next 3 ingredients in a heavy saucepan over low heat, stirring constantly, until chocolate melts. Cool.

✦ **Beat** remaining ¾ cup whipping cream, powdered sugar, and vanilla at high speed with an electric mixer until stiff peaks form; fold into chocolate mixture. Cover and chill at least 30 minutes. **Yield:** 2½ cups.

White Chocolate Mousse

½ cup whipping cream, divided
3 (1-ounce) white chocolate baking squares
2 tablespoons light corn syrup

2 tablespoons butter
1 tablespoon powdered sugar
¼ teaspoon vanilla extract

✦ **Cook** 2 tablespoons whipping cream and next 3 ingredients in a heavy saucepan, stirring constantly, over low heat until smooth. Cool.
✦ **Beat** remaining whipping cream, powdered sugar, and vanilla at high speed with an electric mixer until stiff peaks form; fold into white chocolate mixture. **Yield:** 1¼ cups.

Chocolate Ganache

1 (8-ounce) package semisweet chocolate squares

¼ cup whipping cream

✦ **Cook** chocolate and whipping cream in a heavy saucepan over low heat, stirring constantly, until chocolate melts. **Yield:** ¾ cup.

Chocolate-Almond Torte

1 cup whole almonds, toasted
2 tablespoons sugar
2 tablespoons vegetable oil
¾ cup butter or margarine
½ cup whipping cream
4 (4-ounce) bittersweet or semisweet
    chocolate bars, finely chopped

6 large eggs, separated
⅓ cup sugar
1 cup whipping cream
2 tablespoons sugar
3 tablespoons almond liqueur
Garnish: toasted sliced almonds

✦ **Butter** and flour a 9-inch springform pan. Line with wax paper; butter paper.
✦ **Process** ½ cup whole almonds and 2 tablespoons sugar in a food processor until ground. Spoon into a bowl. Process remaining ½ cup whole almonds and oil in food processor 3 minutes or until a thick paste forms, stopping often to scrape down sides.
✦ **Bring** butter and ½ cup whipping cream to a boil in a heavy saucepan over medium heat. Remove from heat, and whisk in chocolate until smooth. Stir in almond mixtures; cool slightly.
✦ **Beat** egg whites at high speed with an electric mixer until foamy. Add ⅓ cup sugar, 1 tablespoon at a time, beating until stiff peaks form and sugar dissolves (2 to 4 minutes). Beat egg yolks until thick and pale. Gradually add chocolate mixture to yolks, beating until blended. Fold in one-third of egg whites. Gradually fold in remaining egg whites. Pour batter into prepared pan.
✦ **Bake** at 350° for 35 minutes or until almost set. Cool on a wire rack. Run a sharp knife around edges to loosen. Remove sides of pan. Chill up to 3 days.
✦ **Beat** 1 cup whipping cream at medium speed with an electric mixer until foamy; gradually add 2 tablespoons sugar, beating until soft peaks form. Stir in liqueur. Serve over torte; garnish, if desired. **Yield:** 1 (9-inch) torte.

Beverle Grieco
Houston, Texas

Tiramisu

⅔ cup sugar
3 cups whipping cream, divided
2 large eggs
2 egg yolks
1 tablespoon all-purpose flour
½ vanilla bean, split
1 (16-ounce) package mascarpone
    cheese

¾ cup brewed espresso
3 tablespoons Marsala
1 (7-ounce) package dried ladyfingers
    (we tested with Bellino Savoiardi)
3 tablespoons powdered sugar
1 tablespoon cocoa

✦ **Stir** together sugar, 2 cups whipping cream, and next 4 ingredients in a heavy saucepan. Cook over medium heat, stirring constantly, 20 minutes or until mixture is thickened. Cool completely. Discard vanilla bean. Whisk in mascarpone.

✦ **Stir** together espresso and Marsala. Dip each ladyfinger into espresso mixture, and place in a 13- x 9-inch dish. Pour mascarpone mixture over ladyfingers.

✦ **Beat** remaining 1 cup whipping cream at high speed with an electric mixer until foamy; gradually add powdered sugar, beating until soft peaks form. Spoon over mascarpone mixture, and sprinkle with cocoa. Cover and chill 2 hours. **Yield:** 10 servings.

Note: You can prepare espresso by stirring together 1 cup hot water and ½ cup ground espresso coffee. Let stand 5 minutes; pour through a wire-mesh strainer, lined with a coffee filter, into a glass measuring cup, discarding coffee grounds. Yield: ¾ cup.

Lynne Faulkner
Anzio, Italy

Lynne Faulkner's Southern recipes have changed since she moved with her husband, Tim, to Italy. Just as Southerners share recipes hand to hand, Lynne has been inspired in Italy by a grandmotherly friend. Here is her version of Tiramisu, a traditional Italian dessert.

Pumpkin Flan

1 cup sugar, divided	1 cup canned pumpkin
2½ cups fat-free milk	1 teaspoon ground cinnamon
3 large eggs	1 teaspoon vanilla extract
3 egg whites	¼ cup flaked coconut

✦ **Sprinkle** ½ cup sugar in a 9-inch round cakepan. Cook over medium-high heat, shaking pan occasionally (using oven mitts), until sugar melts and turns light golden; set aside. (Mixture may crack slightly as it cools.)

✦ **Heat** milk and remaining ½ cup sugar in a heavy saucepan, stirring constantly, until hot and frothy.

✦ **Beat** eggs, egg whites, and next 3 ingredients at medium speed with an electric mixer until blended; gradually add hot milk mixture, beating at low speed.

✦ **Pour** over caramelized sugar. Place cakepan in a roasting pan. Pour hot water into roasting pan to a depth of 1 inch.

✦ **Bake** at 350° for 1 hour or until a knife inserted in center comes out clean.

✦ **Remove** pan from water; cool on a wire rack. Cover and chill.

✦ **Bake** coconut in a shallow pan at 350°, stirring occasionally, 5 to 6 minutes or until toasted. Cool.

✦ **Loosen** edges of flan with a spatula; invert onto a serving plate. Sprinkle with coconut. **Yield:** 8 servings.

Patricia Agnew
Charleston, South Carolina

Black-and-White Crème Brûlée

2½ cups whipping cream, divided
5 (1-ounce) semisweet chocolate
    squares
6 egg yolks

½ cup sugar
1 teaspoon vanilla extract
6 tablespoons light brown sugar

✦ **Cook** ½ cup whipping cream and chocolate in a heavy saucepan over low heat, stirring constantly, until chocolate melts and mixture is smooth. Pour into a large bowl. Whisk together remaining 2 cups whipping cream, yolks, ½ cup sugar, and vanilla until sugar dissolves and mixture is smooth.

✦ **Whisk** 1 cup egg mixture into chocolate mixture until smooth. Cover and chill remaining egg mixture.

✦ **Pour** chocolate mixture evenly into 6 (8-ounce) custard cups; place cups in a 13- x 9-inch pan. Add hot water to pan to depth of ½ inch.

✦ **Bake** at 325° for 30 minutes or until almost set. (Center will be soft.) Slowly pour remaining yolk mixture evenly over custards. Bake 20 to 25 more minutes or until set. Cool custards in water in pan on a wire rack. Remove from pan; cover and chill at least 8 hours.

✦ **Sprinkle** each custard with 1 tablespoon brown sugar; place custards in a pan. Broil 5½ inches from heat (with electric oven door partially open) until sugar melts (about 2 minutes). Let stand 5 minutes to allow sugar to harden. **Yield:** 6 servings.

Nancy Guillemart
Saumur, France

Banana Pudding Trifle

1⅓ cups sugar
¾ cup all-purpose flour
½ teaspoon salt
4 cups milk
8 egg yolks
1 tablespoon vanilla extract
1 (12-ounce) package vanilla wafers

¼ cup bourbon
2 tablespoons rum
6 ripe bananas, sliced
6 (1.4-ounce) English toffee candy
    bars, crushed
2 cups whipping cream
2 tablespoons sifted powdered sugar

✦ **Combine** first 3 ingredients in a large heavy saucepan; whisk in milk. Bring to a boil over medium heat, whisking constantly. Remove from heat.

✦ **Beat** egg yolks until thick and pale. Gradually stir one-fourth of hot mixture into yolks; add to remaining hot mixture, stirring constantly. Cook, stirring constantly, 1 minute. Stir in vanilla.

✦ **Layer** one-third of wafers in a 16-cup trifle bowl or 4-quart baking dish. Combine bourbon and rum; brush over wafers. Top with one-third of banana.

✦ **Spoon** one-third of custard over banana, and sprinkle with ⅓ cup crushed candy bar. Repeat layers twice.

✦ **Beat** cream at medium speed with an electric mixer until foamy; gradually add powdered sugar, beating until soft peaks form. Spread over trifle; sprinkle with remaining crushed candy. Cover; chill 3 hours. **Yield:** 10 to 12 servings.

Beverle Grieco
Houston, Texas

This creamy banana dessert is one of Beverle Grieco's favorite parts of her annual holiday menu. "I especially love the banana pudding," she says. "It's so Southern."

Turn to page 150 to find Beverle's complete menu.

Cookies 'n' Cream Dessert

½ gallon vanilla ice cream
8 ounces chocolate-flavored candy
    coating, melted
½ cup finely chopped Sugar-and-Spice
    Pecans (see recipe on page 8)

½ teaspoon edible gold-leaf
    powder
24 star-shaped sugar cookies

✦ **Scoop** ice cream into 12 balls onto a cookie sheet; place in freezer.

✦ **Place** melted candy coating in a small heavy-duty, zip-top plastic bag. Snip a small hole in 1 corner of bag; drizzle inside of 12 goblets to decorate. Set goblets aside in a cool, dry place. (Do not store in refrigerator.)

✦ **Place** an ice cream ball in each glass. Sprinkle ice cream with Sugar-and-Spice Pecans and gold-leaf powder; top with cookies. **Yield:** 12 servings.

Note: For cookies, roll a 20-ounce package of refrigerated sugar cookie dough to ⅛-inch thickness on a lightly floured surface. Cut into star shapes, using star-shaped cookie cutters that have been dipped in flour. Bake on greased cookie sheets at 350° for 7 minutes. Yield: about 5 dozen cookies.

Santa's Favorite Cookies and Candies

Signal the start of the Christmas season with batches of old-fashioned sweets. ✦ Try Fruitcake Cookies (page 128) for a traditional holiday treat. Packed with pecans, dates, and candied cherries, they're irresistible. ✦ Capture a child's imagination with a cookie-painting party featuring Nutcracker Cookies (page 131). Decorating them is almost as much fun as devouring them. ✦ Satisfy a chocolate craving with decadent Chocolate-Praline Truffles (page 136) or one of its variations. ✦ With cookies and candies as easy and delicious as these, your only challenge will be saving some for Santa.

Clockwise from top left: Chess Brownies, page 133; Nutcracker Cookie, page 131; White Chocolate-Praline Truffles, page 136; Millionaires, page 135; Mom Ford's Chocolate Chip Cookies, page 126; Chocolate-Praline Truffles, page 136

Almond Cookies

Joey and Stacy Rabon named their cozy bakery "Kudzu" because "we planned to take over the world," Joey laughs. Instead, they have taken over the hearts and the stomachs of their clientele with such specialties as Almond Cookies.

¾ cup sugar
¼ cup all-purpose flour
2½ cups sliced almonds

1 egg white, lightly beaten
⅓ cup butter, melted
1 teaspoon vanilla extract

✦ **Stir** together first 3 ingredients in a large bowl; add egg white, butter, and vanilla, stirring well.
✦ **Drop** dough by tablespoonfuls onto parchment paper-lined cookie sheets.
✦ **Bake** at 350° for 10 to 12 minutes or until golden.
✦ **Cool** on cookie sheets. Remove from paper; store in an airtight container. **Yield:** 2½ dozen.

Joey and Stacy Rabon
Georgetown, South Carolina

Mom Ford's Chocolate Chip Cookies

(pictured on page 124)

Gary Ford's mom first made these cookies soon after Nestlé introduced chocolate morsels in 1939. Gary has preserved the recipe in high-tech fashion—on his personal computer.

½ cup shortening
⅓ cup sugar
⅓ cup firmly packed brown sugar
1 large egg
½ teaspoon vanilla extract
1 cup all-purpose flour

½ teaspoon baking soda
¼ teaspoon salt
1 cup (6 ounces) semisweet
   chocolate morsels
½ cup chopped pecans

✦ **Beat** shortening at medium speed with an electric mixer until fluffy. Gradually add sugars, beating mixture well. Add egg and vanilla, beating until blended.
✦ **Stir** together flour, soda, and salt; add to shortening mixture, mixing well. Stir in chocolate morsels and pecans.
✦ **Drop** dough by tablespoonfuls onto ungreased cookie sheets.
✦ **Bake** at 350° for 10 to 12 minutes. Transfer to wire racks to cool. **Yield:** 2 dozen.

Gary Ford
Birmingham, Alabama

Chocolate-Caramel Thumbprints

A gooey caramel center guarantees these will disappear quickly from the platter.

½ cup butter or margarine, softened
½ cup sugar
2 (1-ounce) semisweet chocolate
    squares, melted
1 egg yolk
2 teaspoons vanilla extract
1¼ cups all-purpose flour
¼ teaspoon baking soda

¼ teaspoon salt
¾ cup very finely chopped pecans
16 milk caramels, unwrapped (we
    tested with Brach's)
2½ tablespoons whipping cream
⅔ cup semisweet chocolate morsels
2 teaspoons shortening

✦ **Beat** butter at medium speed with an electric mixer until creamy; gradually add sugar, beating well. Add melted chocolate and egg yolk, beating until blended. Stir in vanilla. Stir together flour, soda, and salt; add to butter mixture, beating well. Cover and chill 1 hour.

✦ **Shape** dough into 1-inch balls; roll balls in pecans. Place balls 1 inch apart on greased cookie sheets. Press thumb gently into center of each ball, leaving an indentation. Bake at 350° for 12 minutes or until set. Combine caramels and cream in top of a double boiler over simmering water. Cook over medium-low heat, stirring constantly, until caramels melt and mixture is smooth.

✦ **Remove** cookies from oven; cool slightly, and press center of each cookie again. Quickly spoon ¾ teaspoon caramel mixture into center of each cookie. Transfer to wire racks to cool.

✦ **Place** morsels and shortening in a heavy-duty, zip-top plastic bag; seal. Microwave at HIGH 1 to 1½ minutes; squeeze bag until chocolate melts. Snip a tiny hole in 1 corner of bag; drizzle over cooled cookies. **Yield:** about 2½ dozen.

Oatmeal-Molasses Cookies

(pictured on facing page)

2 cups sugar	1 teaspoon baking soda
1 cup vegetable oil	1 teaspoon salt
⅓ cup molasses	1 teaspoon ground cinnamon
2 large eggs	2 cups quick-cooking oats, uncooked
2 cups all-purpose flour	1 cup raisins
1 teaspoon baking powder	1 cup flaked coconut (optional)

✦ **Beat** first 4 ingredients in a large mixing bowl at medium speed with an electric beater until smooth.

✦ **Stir** together flour and next 4 ingredients. Add to sugar mixture, mixing well. Stir in oats, raisins, and, if desired, coconut.

✦ **Drop** dough by heaping teaspoonfuls onto lightly greased cookie sheets.

✦ **Bake** at 350° for 10 minutes. Cool slightly on cookie sheets; transfer to wire racks to cool completely. **Yield:** about 6 dozen.

Fruitcake Cookies

Carrie Treichel says that she has been making these cookies during the holidays since 1949 "because everyone likes them so much." Her version of fruitcake cookies features pecans, dates, and candied cherries.

½ cup shortening	½ teaspoon baking powder
1 cup firmly packed light brown sugar	½ teaspoon salt
1 large egg	1 cup chopped dates
¼ cup buttermilk	1 cup chopped pecans
2 cups all-purpose flour	1 cup chopped candied cherries
½ teaspoon baking soda	5 dozen pecan halves (optional)

✦ **Stir** together first 3 ingredients in a large bowl; stir in buttermilk.

✦ **Stir** together flour and next 3 ingredients; stir into brown sugar mixture. Stir in dates, pecans, and cherries; cover and chill 1 hour.

✦ **Drop** dough by rounded teaspoonfuls 2 inches apart onto lightly greased cookie sheets. Top each cookie with a pecan half, if desired.

✦ **Bake** at 375° for 10 minutes or until lightly browned. Transfer to wire racks to cool. **Yield:** 5 dozen.

Carrie Treichel
Johnson City, Tennessee

Oatmeal-Molasses
Cookies

Rum-Currant Shortbread

Native Southerner
Marty Wingate features
make-ahead recipes at
her annual holiday
open house because
they allow her to be in
the thick of the party.
Her cookies on this
page—Rum-Currant
Shortbread and Brown
Sugar Shortbread—can
be frozen and enjoyed
anytime.

½ cup currants
¼ cup light rum
1 cup butter, softened
½ cup sifted powdered sugar

1¾ cups all-purpose flour
¼ teaspoon baking powder
¼ teaspoon salt

✦ **Bring** currants and rum to a boil in a small saucepan; remove from heat. Cover and let stand 30 minutes; drain. Beat butter at medium speed with an electric mixer until creamy; gradually add sugar, beating well. Stir together flour, baking powder, and salt; gradually add to butter mixture, beating at low speed until blended after each addition. Stir in currants. Cover; chill 30 minutes.
✦ **Roll** dough to ¼-inch thickness on a lightly floured surface. Cut with a 2-inch round cutter; place 2 inches apart on lightly greased cookie sheets. Bake at 375° for 12 to 14 minutes or until edges just begin to brown; cool on cookie sheets on wire racks 5 minutes. Transfer to wire racks to cool. **Yield:** 2 dozen.

Marty Wingate
Seattle, Washington

Brown Sugar Shortbread

(pictured on page 20)

1 cup butter, softened
½ cup firmly packed brown sugar

2 cups all-purpose flour
2 to 3 tablespoons white sparkling sugar

✦ **Beat** butter at medium speed with an electric mixer until creamy; gradually add brown sugar, beating until light and fluffy. Gradually add flour, beating at low speed until smooth. Cover; chill 30 minutes. Roll dough to ¼-inch thickness on a lightly floured surface. Cut with a 2-inch triangle-shaped cutter; place 1 inch apart on lightly greased cookie sheets. Sprinkle with sparkling sugar. Bake at 375° for 10 to 12 minutes or until edges are golden; cool on cookie sheets on wire racks 5 minutes. Transfer to wire racks to cool. **Yield:** about 1½ dozen.

Marty Wingate
Seattle, Washington

Pecan Crescent Cookies

1 cup butter or margarine, cut up
2 cups all-purpose flour
1 cup cottage cheese

¼ cup butter or margarine, melted
1½ cups firmly packed brown sugar
1 cup chopped pecans

✦ **Cut** 1 cup butter into flour with a pastry blender until crumbly. Stir in cheese until blended. Divide dough into thirds; wrap each portion separately in plastic wrap. Chill 2 hours. Roll each portion into a 10-inch circle on a well-floured surface (dough will be sticky). Brush with butter; sprinkle with brown sugar. Top with pecans. Lightly press sugar and pecans into dough with a rolling pin.

✦ **Cut** each circle into quarters. Cut each quarter into 4 wedges, and roll up, starting with long end; place, point side down, on ungreased cookie sheets.

✦ **Bake** at 350° for 30 minutes or until lightly browned. Transfer immediately to wire racks to cool. **Yield:** 4 dozen.

Lea Snell
Florence, Alabama

Nutcracker Cookies

(pictured on page 124)

2 cups butter or margarine, softened
1 cup sugar
3 egg yolks
4¼ cups all-purpose flour
¼ teaspoon baking powder

¼ teaspoon salt
2 teaspoons vanilla extract
1 teaspoon almond extract
Powdered Sugar Paints

✦ **Beat** butter at medium speed with an electric mixer until creamy; gradually add sugar, beating well. Add egg yolks, one at a time, beating until blended after each addition.

✦ **Stir** together flour, baking powder, and salt; gradually add to butter mixture, beating at low speed until blended after each addition. Stir in flavorings. Divide dough in half; wrap each portion in plastic wrap. Chill at least 4 hours.

✦ **Roll** 1 portion at a time to ¼-inch thickness on a lightly floured surface. Cut with a 7-inch toy soldier cutter or other Christmas cookie cutter; place 2 inches apart on lightly greased cookie sheets.

✦ **Bake** at 350° for 15 minutes or until edges are golden. Cool on cookie sheets on wire racks 3 minutes; transfer to wire racks to cool.

✦ **Decorate** with Powdered Sugar Paints, using a small spatula or paintbrush. **Yield:** 1½ dozen.

Powdered Sugar Paints

3 cups sifted powdered sugar
2 tablespoons light corn syrup
2 to 3 tablespoons milk

1 teaspoon vanilla extract
Assorted food colorings

✦ **Stir** together sugar and syrup; stir in milk and vanilla to desired spreading consistency. Place mixture evenly in several small bowls; stir drops of a different food coloring into each bowl. **Yield:** about 3 cups.

Jan Faucette
Tuscaloosa, Alabama

Like every grand-mother, Jan Faucette knows Christmas is for children. Celebrating with her grandchildren is something she looks forward to all year.

One year she held a nutcracker-themed party for her grand-children and their friends. Jan recruited a few gracious moms to help make these cookies for the kids to adorn. The result was a fairyland of sweets—and a Christmas memory that Jan and the children will cherish for a lifetime.

Cranberry-Caramel Bars

1 cup fresh cranberries
2 tablespoons sugar
2 cups all-purpose flour
½ teaspoon baking soda
2 cups uncooked regular oats
½ cup sugar
½ cup firmly packed light brown sugar
1 cup butter or margarine, melted
1 (10-ounce) package chopped dates
¾ cup chopped pecans
1 (12-ounce) jar caramel sauce
⅓ cup all-purpose flour

✦ **Stir** together cranberries and 2 tablespoons sugar in a small bowl; set aside.
✦ **Stir** together 2 cups flour and next 4 ingredients; stir in butter until crumbly. Reserve 1 cup flour mixture. Press remaining mixture into bottom of a lightly greased 13- x 9-inch baking dish.
✦ **Bake** at 350° for 15 minutes. Sprinkle with dates, pecans, and cranberry mixture. Stir together caramel sauce and ⅓ cup flour; spoon over top. Sprinkle with reserved 1 cup flour mixture. Bake 20 more minutes or until lightly browned. Cool on a wire rack. Cut into bars. **Yield:** 2 dozen.

Patsy Butler
Houston, Texas

Hermits

Sugar and spice and everything nice make up these chewy bar cookies.

1½ cups sugar
½ cup vegetable oil
½ cup molasses
2 large eggs
2½ cups all-purpose flour
1 teaspoon baking soda

½ teaspoon ground cinnamon
½ teaspoon ground nutmeg
½ teaspoon ground cloves
½ teaspoon ground ginger
1 cup raisins

✦ **Combine** first 3 ingredients in a large mixing bowl; beat at medium speed with an electric mixer until well blended. Add eggs, one at at time, beating well after each addition.

✦ **Stir** together flour and next 5 ingredients; gradually add to sugar mixture, beating well. Stir in raisins. Spread batter evenly into a lightly greased 15- x 10-inch jellyroll pan.

✦ **Bake** at 350° for 25 minutes. Cool slightly in pan on a wire rack. Cut into bars. **Yield:** 32 bars.

Chess Brownies

(pictured on page 124)

A box of cake mix makes quick work of these blond brownies studded with pecans and topped with a soft cream cheese layer.

1 cup chopped pecans
½ cup butter, melted
3 large eggs
1 (18.25-ounce) package yellow
    cake mix

1 (8-ounce) package cream cheese,
    softened
1 (16-ounce) package powdered
    sugar

✦ **Stir** together pecans, butter, 1 egg, and cake mix until well blended; press in bottom of a lightly greased 13- x 9-inch pan. Set aside.

✦ **Combine** remaining 2 eggs, cream cheese, and powdered sugar in a large mixing bowl; beat at medium speed with an electric mixer until smooth. Pour cream cheese mixture over cake mix layer.

✦ **Bake** at 325° for 40 minutes or until cheese mixture is set. Cool completely in pan on a wire rack. Cut into squares. **Yield:** 15 brownies.

Chewy Scotch Bars

Treat your family to these chewy, chocolaty bars—a specialty of Lynda Borden's. They get their butterscotch flavor from the irresistible butter-brown sugar combination.

2 cups (12 ounces) semisweet chocolate morsels
2 tablespoons butter or margarine
1 (14-ounce) can sweetened condensed milk
1 cup butter or margarine, melted

1 (16-ounce) package light brown sugar
2 large eggs, lightly beaten
2 cups all-purpose flour
½ teaspoon salt
1 teaspoon vanilla extract
1 cup chopped pecans

✦ **Microwave** first 3 ingredients in a 2-quart microwave-safe bowl at HIGH 1½ minutes or until chocolate and butter melt, stirring twice.

✦ **Stir** together 1 cup melted butter and brown sugar. Add eggs, stirring until blended.

✦ **Stir** in chocolate mixture, flour, and remaining ingredients. Pour batter into a greased 15- x 10-inch jellyroll pan.

✦ **Bake** at 350° for 30 minutes or until a wooden pick inserted in center comes out clean (do not overbake). Cool in pan on a wire rack; cut into bars. Serve with ice cream, if desired. **Yield:** 2½ dozen.

Lynda Borden
Shreveport, Louisiana

Caramel-Pecan Logs

1 (13-ounce) jar marshmallow creme
1 teaspoon vanilla extract
1 to 2 (16-ounce) packages powdered
    sugar, sifted
1 tablespoon milk

2 (14-ounce) packages caramels,
    unwrapped (we tested with
    Farley)
4 cups chopped pecans, toasted

✦ **Stir** together marshmallow creme and vanilla in a large bowl. Grease hands with shortening; gradually knead enough powdered sugar into marshmallow cream mixture until consistency is stiff.

✦ **Divide** mixture into 4 portions. Shape each portion into a 6-inch log. Wrap in plastic wrap, and freeze 1 hour. (Logs should be hard.)

✦ **Combine** milk and caramels in a large heavy skillet; cook over medium-low heat until caramels melt and mixture is smooth, stirring often.

✦ **Dip** each log into caramel mixture; working quickly, roll in pecans, and wrap in plastic wrap. Store in refrigerator or freeze up to 1 month. To serve, cut into ¼-inch slices. **Yield:** 4 (6-inch) logs.

Millionaires

(pictured on page 124)

1 (14-ounce) package caramels,
    unwrapped (we tested with
    Farley)
2 tablespoons milk

2 cups chopped pecans
2 cups (12 ounces) semisweet
    chocolate morsels

✦ **Combine** caramels and milk in a heavy saucepan; cook mixture over medium-low heat, stirring often, until smooth. Stir in pecans, and drop by teaspoonfuls onto buttered cookie sheets. Let stand until firm.

✦ **Microwave** chocolate in a 1-quart microwave-safe bowl at HIGH 1 minute or until melted, stirring once.

✦ **Dip** caramel candies into melted chocolate, allowing excess to drip; place on buttered cookie sheets. Let candy stand until firm. **Yield:** 34 candies.

Cheryl Hughes
El Dorado, Arkansas

Chocolate-Praline Truffles

(pictured on page 124)

This recipe's decadent truffle mixture—chocolate, whipping cream, butter, and almond liqueur—is wonderful when shaped into balls and rolled in sugared pecans. But it also adds richness to Chocolate Truffle Cake (page 110), where it is spread on the cake layers as a ganache.

1½ cups chopped pecans
¼ cup firmly packed light brown sugar
2 tablespoons whipping cream
3 (4-ounce) semisweet chocolate bars,
     broken into pieces (we tested with
     Ghirardelli)

¼ cup whipping cream
3 tablespoons butter, cut up
2 tablespoons almond liqueur

✦ **Stir** together first 3 ingredients; spread in a lightly buttered 9-inch round cakepan.

✦ **Bake** at 350° for 20 minutes or until coating appears slightly crystallized, stirring once. Remove from oven; stir and cool.

✦ **Microwave** chocolate and ¼ cup whipping cream in a 2-quart microwave-safe bowl at MEDIUM (50% power) 3½ minutes.

✦ **Whisk** until chocolate melts and mixture is smooth. (If chocolate doesn't melt completely, microwave and whisk at 15 second intervals until melted.) Whisk in butter and liqueur; let stand 20 minutes.

✦ **Beat** at medium speed with an electric mixer 4 minutes or until soft peaks form. (Do not overbeat.) Cover and chill at least 4 hours.

✦ **Shape** mixture into 1-inch balls; roll in pecans. Cover and chill up to 1 week, or freeze up to 1 month. **Yield:** about 2 dozen.

White Chocolate-Praline Truffles (pictured on page 124): Substitute 3 (4-ounce) white chocolate bars for semisweet chocolate bars and almonds for pecans.

Chocolate-Marble Truffles: Prepare 1 recipe each of mixture for Chocolate-Praline Truffles and mixture for White Chocolate-Praline Truffles. Spoon both mixtures into a 13- x 9-inch pan; swirl with a knife. Chill and shape as directed; roll in cream-filled chocolate sandwich cookie crumbs, omitting pecan mixture.

Buttermilk Fudge

Butter or margarine
2 cups sugar
1 cup buttermilk
½ cup butter or margarine

1 teaspoon baking soda
2 tablespoons light corn syrup
1 teaspoon vanilla extract
¾ cup chopped pecans, toasted

✦ **Butter** a Dutch oven. Stir together sugar and next 4 ingredients in Dutch oven.
✦ **Cook** over medium heat, stirring constantly, until a candy thermometer registers 234° (soft ball stage). Remove from heat. Cool to 180°. Stir in vanilla.
✦ **Beat** at high speed with an electric mixer until mixture thickens and begins to lose its gloss. Stir in pecans.
✦ **Pour** into a buttered 8-inch square pan or dish. Cool completely. Cut into squares. **Yield:** 1¼ pounds.

Terri Abbott
Bartlesville, Oklahoma

Chocolate Fudge

1 tablespoon butter or margarine
4½ cups sugar
1 (12-ounce) can evaporated milk
2 tablespoons butter or margarine
¼ teaspoon salt
2 cups milk chocolate morsels

2 cups (12 ounces) semisweet
    chocolate morsels
1 (13-ounce) jar marshmallow
    creme
1 teaspoon vanilla extract
2 cups chopped pecans, toasted

✦ **Butter** a large heavy saucepan with 1 tablespoon butter. Stir together sugar and next 3 ingredients in pan.
✦ **Cook** over medium heat, stirring constantly, until sugar dissolves and mixture comes to a boil.
✦ **Cook,** covered, 2 to 3 minutes to wash down sugar crystals from sides of pan. Uncover and cook, without stirring, until a candy thermometer registers 236° (soft ball stage). Remove from heat.
✦ **Stir** together milk mixture, milk chocolate morsels, semisweet chocolate morsels, and marshmallow creme in a large mixing bowl; beat at medium speed with an electric mixer until smooth. Add vanilla; beat until mixture thickens and begins to lose its gloss (about 10 minutes). Stir in pecans. Quickly pour into a buttered 13- x 9-inch dish. Cool completely. Cut into squares. **Yield:** 5 pounds.

Gifts from the Kitchen

*S*hare the Christmas spirit with homemade gifts from

your kitchen. You'll brighten someone's day while

saving yourself some time and money. ✦ Help out friends

who have company coming by offering them Cream Cheese

Braids (page 140). The recipe yields four delicious loaves

that are perfect as part of a holiday breakfast. ✦ Simplify

your schedule by giving Slow Cooker Apple Butter (page

143). Just toss apple slices, cider vinegar, sugar, and nutmeg

into your slow cooker. Then turn it on and forget about it

until the apple butter is done. ✦ Fill holiday gift tins with

the quick candies on pages 146 and 147. Just make a batch

of each candy, and then mix and match them for variety.

Holiday gift-giving has never been easier!

Rum Balls, page 147

Cream Cheese Braids

1 (8-ounce) container sour cream
½ cup sugar
½ cup butter or margarine, cut into
    pieces
1 teaspoon salt
2 (¼-ounce) envelopes active dry yeast
½ cup warm water (105° to 115°)

2 large eggs, lightly beaten
4 cups all-purpose flour
Cream Cheese Filling (see facing page)
2½ cups sifted powdered sugar
¼ cup milk
2 teaspoons vanilla extract

✦ **Heat** first 4 ingredients in a saucepan, stirring occasionally, until butter melts. Cool to 105° to 115°.

✦ **Combine** yeast and warm water in a large mixing bowl; let stand 5 minutes.

✦ **Stir** in sour cream mixture and eggs; gradually stir in flour (dough will be soft). Cover and chill at least 8 hours.

✦ **Divide** dough into fourths. Turn each portion out onto a heavily floured surface; knead 4 or 5 times. Roll each portion into a 12- x 8-inch rectangle; spread each rectangle with one-fourth of Cream Cheese Filling, leaving a 1-inch border around edges. Carefully roll up rectangles, starting at a long side; press seams, and fold ends under to seal.

✦ **Place,** seam side down, on lightly greased baking sheets. Cut 6 equally spaced Xs across top of each loaf; cover and let rise in a warm place (85°), free from drafts, about 1 hour or until doubled in bulk. Bake at 375° for 15 to 20 minutes or until browned. Stir together sugar, milk, and vanilla; drizzle glaze over warm loaves. (If desired, freeze baked braids without glaze; thaw in refrigerator, and drizzle with glaze before serving.) **Yield:** 4 (12-inch) loaves.

Cream Cheese Filling

2 (8-ounce) packages cream cheese, softened

¾ cup sugar

1 large egg

2 teaspoons vanilla extract

✦ **Place** all ingredients in a medium bowl; beat at medium speed with an electric mixer until smooth. **Yield:** about 2½ cups.

Jambalaya Mix

1 cup uncooked long-grain rice (we tested with Uncle Ben's Converted Rice)

1 tablespoon instant minced onion

1 tablespoon green pepper flakes

1 tablespoon dried parsley flakes

2 teaspoons beef bouillon granules

½ teaspoon garlic powder

½ teaspoon ground black pepper

¼ teaspoon dried thyme

⅛ to ¼ teaspoon dried crushed red pepper

1 bay leaf

✦ **Combine** all ingredients; store in an airtight container. **Yield:** 1½ cups.

Jambalaya: Bring Jambalaya Mix, 3 cups water, and 1 (8-ounce) can tomato sauce to a boil in a Dutch oven. Stir in 1 cup chopped cooked chicken and 1 cup chopped cooked ham or smoked sausage. Cover, reduce heat, and simmer 20 to 25 minutes or until rice is tender. Discard bay leaf. Yield: about 8 cups.

Linda Jordan
Little Rock, Arkansas

Southwestern Black Bean-Corn Salsa

2 teaspoons cumin seeds

4 (15-ounce) cans black beans, rinsed and drained

2 (15¼-ounce) cans whole kernel corn, drained

2 red bell peppers, minced

1 purple onion, minced

1 cup minced fresh cilantro

1 cup minced fresh parsley

⅔ cup lime juice

½ cup olive oil

6 garlic cloves, pressed

2 teaspoons dried crushed red pepper

1 teaspoon ground black pepper

✦ **Cook** cumin seeds in a small cast-iron skillet over medium heat 2 to 3 minutes or until browned, stirring often. Stir together cumin seeds, black beans, and remaining ingredients; toss well. Cover and store in refrigerator up to 2 weeks. Serve with tortilla chips, fajitas, fish, or steak. **Yield:** 10 cups.

Sheila Fogle
Huntsville, Alabama

Slow Cooker Apple Butter

Slow Cooker Apple Butter

(pictured on facing page)

4 pounds cooking apples, peeled and
    sliced
½ cup apple cider vinegar

3 cups sugar
1 cup firmly packed brown sugar
1 teaspoon ground nutmeg

✦ **Place** apple slices and vinegar in a 4-quart slow cooker.

✦ **Cook,** covered, at HIGH 6 hours. Stir in sugars and nutmeg. Reduce setting
to LOW, and cook, covered, 4 hours. Cool. Store butter in refrigerator up to
1 week. Serve with breakfast breads. **Yield:** 6 cups.

Peggy Fowler Revels
Woodruff, South Carolina

Chili Sauce

This simple sauce from Shirley Hall's ancestor makes a
piquant, zesty addition to black-eyed peas. And it fills up
11 half-pint jars—so you'll have plenty to share as gifts.

4 quarts chopped fresh tomatoes
    (about 7½ pounds)
2 cups chopped onion
3 green bell peppers,
    chopped
2 cups white vinegar
½ cup firmly packed brown
    sugar

2 tablespoons salt
1½ teaspoons dry mustard
1½ teaspoons ground cloves
1½ teaspoons ground
    allspice
1½ teaspoons pepper

✦ **Combine** all ingredients in a large Dutch oven; bring to a boil. Cover, reduce
heat, and simmer 1 hour, stirring occasionally.

✦ **Pour** hot mixture into hot jars, filling to ½ inch from top. Remove air
bubbles, and wipe jar rims. Cover jars at once with metal lids, and screw
on bands.

✦ **Process** in boiling-water bath 15 minutes. **Yield:** 11 half-pints.

Shirley Hall
Ocean City, Maryland

While rummaging through the bottom of a trunk, Shirley Hall discovered a family treasure—a recipe book that belonged to her great-great-grandmother. Shirley now proudly displays her ancestor's original recipe for this tasty Chili Sauce in a frame, using an old-fashioned dish towel as a mat.

Hot Fudge Ice Cream Topping

(pictured below)

Presents from the kitchen mean something special for the giver, too:
freedom from last-minute shopping frenzies. For a gourmet treat,
tuck a jar of this topping in a basket with an ice cream scoop.

2 (1-ounce) semisweet chocolate squares
¾ cup sugar

1 cup evaporated milk
2 tablespoons butter or margarine
1 teaspoon vanilla extract

✦ **Melt** chocolate in a heavy saucepan over low heat.

✦ **Stir** in sugar until smooth. Gradually add milk, stirring until smooth. Bring to a boil over medium heat, stirring constantly.

✦ **Boil,** stirring constantly, 6 minutes. Remove from heat; stir in butter and vanilla. Store in refrigerator up to 3 weeks. Serve warm over ice cream.
Yield: 1½ cups.

Kay Murphy
Austin, Texas

Maple-Pecan Ice Cream Topping, facing page

Hot Fudge

Hot Fudge Ice Cream Topping, above

Maple-Pecan Ice Cream Topping

(pictured on facing page)

¾ cup firmly packed light brown sugar 2 tablespoons butter or margarine
¼ cup water ½ cup chopped pecans, toasted
3 tablespoons maple syrup ¼ cup whipping cream

✦ **Cook** first 3 ingredients in a small saucepan over medium heat, stirring constantly, 6 to 8 minutes or until a candy thermometer registers 234° (soft ball stage). Remove from heat; stir in butter. Cool.
✦ **Stir** in pecans and whipping cream. Store in refrigerator up to 3 weeks. Serve warm over ice cream. **Yield:** 1 cup.

Karie Mitchell
Birmingham, Alabama

Christmas Spritz Cookies

1 cup butter, softened 2½ cups all-purpose flour
1 cup sugar ⅛ teaspoon salt
2 large eggs 10 drops of yellow liquid food coloring
2 teaspoons vanilla extract Red and green decorator candies

✦ **Beat** butter at medium speed with an electric mixer until creamy; gradually add sugar, beating well. Add eggs and vanilla, beating until blended.
✦ **Combine** flour and salt; add to butter mixture, beating at low speed until blended. Add food coloring, beating until blended.
✦ **Use** a cookie gun with a bar-shaped disc to shape dough into 1½-inch cookies following manufacturer's instructions; or shape dough into 1-inch balls, and flatten to ¼-inch thickness with a flat-bottomed glass. Place on greased cookie sheets; sprinkle with candies.
✦ **Bake** at 375° for 8 minutes or until edges are lightly browned. Transfer to wire racks to cool. **Yield:** about 8 dozen.

Bertha Bareuther
Cambridge, Maryland

Bertha Bareuther has been making these cookies at Christmastime since her children were small. "We give containers of them as gifts. Our friends really look forward to them," she says. Real butter gives the cookies their rich flavor.

From left:
Peanut Clusters,
Butterscotch-Peanut
Fudge, Coconut Joys

Butterscotch-Peanut Fudge

(pictured above)

Each holiday season,
Betty Moore uses tried-
and-true recipes to
prepare trays for her
husband's employees.

"I need recipes that
make a large quantity,
are quick, and, most
importantly, are fool-
proof," Betty says. Try
all of her easy confec-
tions (pictured above).

1 (11-ounce) package butterscotch
  morsels
1 (14-ounce) can sweetened
  condensed milk
1½ cups miniature marshmallows

⅔ cup chunky peanut butter
1 teaspoon vanilla extract
⅛ teaspoon salt
1 cup chopped dry-roasted peanuts

✦ **Cook** first 3 ingredients in a small heavy saucepan over medium heat, stirring constantly, 5 minutes or until smooth; remove from heat. Stir in peanut butter, vanilla, and salt until blended; stir in peanuts. Pour into a buttered 9-inch square pan. Chill until firm; cut into squares. Store in refrigerator. **Yield:** 2½ pounds.

Note: If desired, microwave first 3 ingredients in a 2-quart microwave-safe bowl at HIGH 2 to 3 minutes or until melted, stirring twice.

Betty Moore
Kennett Square, Pennsylvania

Coconut Joys

(pictured on facing page)

½ cup butter or margarine
2 cups sifted powdered sugar

3 cups flaked coconut
⅓ cup semisweet chocolate morsels

✦ **Melt** butter in a saucepan over low heat; remove from heat.
✦ **Stir** in sugar and coconut; shape into ¾-inch balls. Chill until firm.
✦ **Place** morsels in a small heavy-duty, zip-top plastic bag; seal. Submerge bag in hot water until chocolate melts. Snip a tiny hole in 1 corner of bag, and drizzle chocolate over coconut balls. Store in refrigerator. **Yield:** 3½ dozen.

Betty Moore
Kennett Square, Pennsylvania

Peanut Clusters

(pictured on facing page)

8 (2-ounce) vanilla candy coating
   squares, cut up

2⅔ cups milk chocolate morsels
1 pound salted Spanish peanuts

✦ **Melt** candy coating and chocolate morsels in a heavy saucepan over low heat, stirring constantly. Remove from heat; stir in peanuts. Drop by table-spoonfuls onto wax paper-lined cookie sheets. Chill until firm. **Yield:** 4 dozen.

Betty Moore
Kennett Square, Pennsylvania

Rum Balls

(pictured on page 138)

1 (12-ounce) package vanilla wafers
1 (16-ounce) package pecan pieces
½ cup honey

⅔ cup dark rum or bourbon
Sifted powdered sugar or vanilla wafer
   crumbs

✦ **Process** wafers in a food processor until crumbs are fine; transfer to a bowl. Process pecans in processor until finely chopped. Stir into wafer crumbs. Stir in honey and rum. Shape into 1-inch balls; roll in sugar or additional wafer crumbs. Store in an airtight container in refrigerator up to 1 month. **Yield:** 6 dozen.

Chocolate-Rum Balls: Substitute 1 (9-ounce) package thin dark chocolate wafer cookies for vanilla wafers. Decrease honey to ⅓ cup and rum to ½ cup. Yield: 5 dozen.

Lela H. Coggins
Brevard, North Carolina

Special Occasion Menus

*M*ake the season's celebrations memorable with one of these 10 scrumptious menus. Each menu takes the guesswork out of meal-planning by grouping recipes from throughout the book and providing their page numbers. Also listed are suggested store-bought items, such as salad or bakery rolls. ✦ Elegant entertaining will be easy with one of the four formal menus that begin on the next page, from Simple-and-Elegant Christmas Dinner to Traditional Turkey Feast. ✦ The casual meals that end the chapter set the scene for cozy gatherings, from decorating the tree to relaxing on the day after Christmas.

Down-home Dinner for Friends, page 153

Simple-and-Elegant Christmas Dinner

.... ◆ ....

Serves Four

Beef Tenderloin Steaks with
Balsamic Sauce, page 71

Garlic-Gruyère Mashed Potatoes,
page 96

Roasted Asparagus with
Red Pepper Sauce, page 92

Bakery rolls

Ultimate Cheesecake, page 113

High-Flavor Holiday Menu

.... ◆ ....

Serves Six to Eight

Carrot-Butternut Squash
Soup, page 64

Beef Tenderloin with Five-Onion
Sauce, page 70

Pistachio Risotto with Saffron,
page 91

Oven-Roasted Potatoes, Green
Beans, and Onions, page 96

Chocolate-Almond Torte, page 120

Banana Pudding Trifle, page 123

Cozy Christmas Eve Entertaining

‧‧‧‧‧‧‧‧‧‧ ◆ ‧‧‧‧‧‧‧‧‧‧

Serves Four

Orange-Ginger Hens with
Cranberry Salsa, page 81

Basmati rice pilaf

Steamed baby carrots

Black-and-White
Crème Brûlée, page 122

Traditional Turkey Feast

‧‧‧‧‧‧‧‧‧‧ ◆ ‧‧‧‧‧‧‧‧‧‧

Serves Eight

Brussels Sprouts with Parmesan
Soufflés, page 94

Wild Rice-Stuffed Turkey Breast,
page 84

Roasted Winter Vegetables, page 97

Buttered Asparagus Spears, page 92

Bakery rolls

Double-Chocolate Bombe, page 118

Southern Brunch
for a Crowd

························· ◆ ·························

Serves Thirty-six

Biscuits and Sausage Gravy,
page 31 (triple the recipe)

Scrambled eggs

Garlic-Cheese Grits, page 28

Fresh fruit

Bakery sweet rolls

Orange juice, hot tea, and coffee

Freezer-Friendly
Menu

················· ◆ ·················

Serves Six

Mixed green salad

Make-Ahead Company
Beef Stew, page 60

Mashed Potato Bowls, page 61

Make-Ahead Crescent Rolls, page 47

Cookies 'n' Cream Dessert,
page 123

Tree-Trimming
Soup Supper

⋯⋯⋯ ◆ ⋯⋯⋯

Serves Six to Eight

Tortellini Tapas with
Spicy Ranch Dip, page 17

White Christmas Chili, page 59

Breadsticks

Mom's Pecan Pie, page 116

Down-home
Dinner for
Friends

⋯⋯⋯ ◆ ⋯⋯⋯

Serves Eight

Timely Fried Chicken, page 58

Dashiell Corn Pudding, page 95

Spicy Green Beans with Purple
Onion, page 93

Hush puppies

Aunt Kitty's Lemon Pie, page 115

Traditional German Holiday

············ ◆ ············

Serves Six

Sauerbraten, page 50

German Potato Pancakes, page 37

German-Style Red Cabbage, page 95

Simple Day-After-Christmas Supper

············ ◆ ············

Serves Four to Six

Leftover roasted chicken, smoked turkey breast, or honey-glazed ham

Broccoli Parmesan, page 93

Sweet Cornbread Dressing, page 88

Cranberry sauce

Bakery rolls

Brownie-Mint Pie, page 117

Metric Equivalents

The recipes that appear in this cookbook use the standard United States method for measuring liquid and dry or solid ingredients (teaspoons, tablespoons, and cups). The information on this chart is provided to help cooks outside the U.S. successfully use these recipes. All equivalents are approximate.

METRIC EQUIVALENTS FOR DIFFERENT TYPES OF INGREDIENTS

A standard cup measure of a dry or solid ingredient will vary in weight depending on the type of ingredient. A standard cup of liquid is the same volume for any type of liquid. Use the following chart when converting standard cup measures to grams (weight) or milliliters (volume).

Standard Cup	Fine Powder (ex. flour)	Grain (ex. rice)	Granular (ex. sugar)	Liquid Solids (ex. butter)	Liquid (ex. milk)
1	140 g	150 g	190 g	200 g	240 ml
¾	105 g	113 g	143 g	150 g	180 ml
⅔	93 g	100 g	125 g	133 g	160 ml
½	70 g	75 g	95 g	100 g	120 ml
⅓	47 g	50 g	63 g	67 g	80 ml
¼	35 g	38 g	48 g	50 g	60 ml
⅛	18 g	19 g	24 g	25 g	30 ml

USEFUL EQUIVALENTS FOR LIQUID INGREDIENTS BY VOLUME

¼ tsp				=	1 ml
½ tsp				=	2 ml
1 tsp				=	5 ml
3 tsp =	1 tbls		= ½ fl oz	=	15 ml
	2 tbls =	⅛ cup	= 1 fl oz	=	30 ml
	4 tbls =	¼ cup	= 2 fl oz	=	60 ml
	5⅓ tbls =	⅓ cup	= 3 fl oz	=	80 ml
	8 tbls =	½ cup	= 4 fl oz	=	120 ml
	10⅔ tbls =	⅔ cup	= 5 fl oz	=	160 ml
	12 tbls =	¾ cup	= 6 fl oz	=	180 ml
	16 tbls =	1 cup	= 8 fl oz	=	240 ml
1 pt =	2 cups	= 16 fl oz	=	480 ml
1 qt =	4 cups	= 32 fl oz	=	960 ml
		33 fl oz	= 1000 ml = 1 l

USEFUL EQUIVALENTS FOR DRY INGREDIENTS BY WEIGHT

(To convert ounces to grams, multiply the number of ounces by 30.)

1 oz	=	1/16 lb	=	30 g
4 oz	=	¼ lb	=	120 g
8 oz	=	½ lb	=	240 g
12 oz	=	¾ lb	=	360 g
16 oz	=	1 lb	=	480 g

USEFUL EQUIVALENTS FOR LENGTH

(To convert inches to centimeters, multiply the number of inches by 2.5.)

1 in =		=	2.5 cm
6 in =	½ ft	=	15 cm
12 in =	1 ft	=	30 cm
36 in =	3 ft = 1 yd	=	90 cm
40 in		=	100 cm = 1 m

USEFUL EQUIVALENTS FOR COOKING/OVEN TEMPERATURES

	Fahrenheit	Celsius	Gas Mark
Freeze Water	32° F	0° C	
Room Temperature	68° F	20° C	
Boil Water	212° F	100° C	
Bake	325° F	160° C	3
	350° F	180° C	4
	375° F	190° C	5
	400° F	200° C	6
	425° F	220° C	7
	450° F	230° C	8
Broil			Grill

Index

Almonds
Cheesecake, Coconut-
Chocolate-Almond, 112
Cookies, Almond, 126
Torte, Chocolate-
Almond, 120
Appetizers
Burritos, Hot Phyllo, 16
Cheese
Ball, Pinecone Cheese, 12
Crostini, Christmas, 13
Puffs, Savory Cheese, 16
Torte, Showstopping
Appetizer, 13
Chicken, Sticky, 18
Dips
Mustard Dip, Sweet-and-
Spicy, 8
Nacho Dip, Layered, 9
Ranch Dip, Tortellini Tapas
with Spicy, 17
Spinach Dip in Sourdough
Round, 10
Flank Steak, Red Wine-
Marinated, 15
Meatballs, Sweet-and-
Sour, 18
Mix, Holiday Party, 8
Pear-Pecan Appetizers, 14
Pecans, Sugar-and-Spice, 8
Shrimp, Marinated, 15
Spreads and Fillings
Feta Cheese Spread, 11
Roasted Red Bell Pepper
Spread, 11
Seafood Spread, Grandma
Reed's, 10
Tapas with Spicy Ranch Dip,
Tortellini, 17
Apples
Butter, Slow Cooker
Apple, 143
Ham and Apples, Grilled, 53
Tenderloin with Praline-Mustard
Glaze, Apple-Stuffed, 75
Applesauce, Chunky, 98
Applesauce Pie, 115
Apricot Glaze, 113
Apricot-Pecan Bread, 36
Asparagus Spears, Buttered, 92
Asparagus with Red Pepper Sauce,
Roasted, 92

Banana Pudding Trifle, 123
Beans
Black Bean-Corn Salsa,
Southwestern, 141
Chili, White Christmas, 59
Green Beans, and Onions,
Oven-Roasted Potatoes, 96
Green Beans with Purple Onion,
Spicy, 93
Red Beans and Rice, New
Orleans, 54
Beef
Reubens, Oven-Grilled, 67
Roasts
Marinated Roast Beef, 50
Rib Roast, Standing, 70
Sauerbraten, 50
Stew, Make-Ahead Company
Beef, 60
Steaks
Flank Steak, Red Wine-
Marinated, 15
Rib-Eye Steaks, Peppered, 72
Tenderloin Steaks with
Balsamic Sauce, Beef, 71
Thai Lemon Beef, 52
Tenderloin with Five-Onion
Sauce, Beef, 70
Beverages
Alcoholic
Coffee, Praline, 19
Eggnog, Southern, 21
Punch, Lemonade-
Bourbon, 21
Cider, Spiced Cranberry, 20
Hot Chocolate, 19
Punch, Sparkling Citrus, 21
Tea, Hot Russian, 19
Biscuits
Cheese Biscuits, Snappy, 38
Sausage Gravy, Biscuits and, 31
Three-Step Biscuits, 39
Blackberry Sauce, Grilled Quail
with Red Wine-, 85
Blueberry Streusel Muffins, 40
Breads. *See also* Biscuits,
Cornbreads, Muffins,
Pancakes, Rolls and Buns.
Apricot-Pecan Bread, 36
Crostini, Christmas, 13
Cumin Bread, 36
Focaccia, Herb, 42

French Toast, Praline, 33
Spoonbread, Corn, 37
Stollen, Easy, 41
Yeast
Braids, Cream Cheese, 140
French Bread, Mom's, 42
Twist, Onion-Poppy Seed, 43
Broccoli and Sausage, Pasta with, 54
Broccoli Parmesan, 93
Brussels Sprouts with Parmesan
Soufflés, 94
Burritos, Hot Phyllo, 16
Butter, Slow Cooker Apple, 143

Cabbage
Coleslaw, Best Barbecue, 102
Red Cabbage, German-Style, 95
Cakes
Carrot Cake, Best, 106
Cheesecake, Coconut-
Chocolate-Almond, 112
Cheesecake, Ultimate, 113
Chocolate Truffle Cake, 110
Coffee Cake, Raspberry-
Cheese, 30
Italian Cream Cake, 107
Pound Cake, Cream Cheese, 111
Red Velvet Peppermint Cake, 108
Torte, Chocolate-Almond, 120
Candies
Balls, Chocolate-Rum, 147
Balls, Rum, 147
Clusters, Peanut, 147
Fudge, Buttermilk, 137
Fudge, Butterscotch-Peanut, 146
Fudge, Chocolate, 137
Joys, Coconut, 147
Logs, Caramel-Pecan, 135
Millionaires, 135
Truffles, Chocolate-Marble, 136
Truffles, Chocolate-Praline, 136
Truffles, White Chocolate-
Praline, 136
Carrot-Butternut Squash Soup, 64
Carrot Cake, Best, 106
Casserole, Egg, 28
Casserole, Sweet Potato-Eggnog, 97
Cheese. *See also* Appetizers/Cheese.
Bake, Hash Brown-Cheese, 28
Biscuits, Snappy Cheese, 38
Braids, Cream Cheese, 140

Broccoli Parmesan, 93
Coffee Cake, Raspberry-
     Cheese, 30
Desserts
    Cake, Cream Cheese
         Pound, 111
    Cheesecake, Coconut-
         Chocolate-Almond, 112
    Cheesecake, Ultimate, 113
    Frosting, Cream
         Cheese, 106
    Frosting, Nutty Cream
         Cheese, 107
    Frosting, Peppermint Cream
         Cheese, 109
    Tiramisu, 120
Filling, Cream Cheese, 141
Grits, Garlic-Cheese, 28
Mashed Potato Bowls, 61
Mashed Potatoes, Garlic-
     Gruyère, 96
Melts, Ham and Cheese, 67
Salad with Feta Cheese and Basil
     Dressing, Spinach, 101
Soufflés, Parmesan, 94
Soup, Mexican Cheese, 64
Cheesecake. See Cakes.
Cherries
Glaze, Cherry, 113
Salad, Congealed Cherry, 99
Sauce, Cherry-Wine, 73
Chicken
Caramelized Chicken with
     Cranberry Conserve, 80
Chili, White Christmas, 59
Dumplings, Chicken and, 57
Fettuccine Supreme,
     Chicken, 57
Fried Chicken, Timely, 58
Greek Chicken Breasts, 79
Imperial Chicken, 81
Jambalaya, 141
Jambalaya, 1-2-3, 53
Roasted Chicken, Easy
     Oven-, 79
Sticky Chicken, 18
Chili, White Christmas, 59
Chocolate
Bars and Cookies
    Chip Cookies, Mom Ford's
         Chocolate, 126
    Scotch Bars, Chewy, 134
    Thumbprints, Chocolate-
         Caramel, 127
Bombe, Double-
     Chocolate, 118

Cakes and Torte
Almond Torte,
     Chocolate-, 120
Cheesecake, Coconut-
     Chocolate-Almond, 112
Truffle Cake, Chocolate, 110
Candies
Balls, Chocolate-Rum, 147
Clusters, Peanut, 147
Fudge, Chocolate, 137
Joys, Coconut, 147
Millionaires, 135
Truffles, Chocolate-
     Marble, 136
Truffles, Chocolate-
     Praline, 136
Truffles, White Chocolate-
     Praline, 136
Crème Brûlée, Black-and-
     White, 122
Frosting and Toppings
Ganache, Chocolate, 119
Ice Cream Topping, Hot
     Fudge, 144
White Chocolate-Buttercream
     Frosting, 111
Hot Chocolate, 19
Mousse, Chocolate, 118
Mousse, White Chocolate, 119
Pies
Brownie-Mint Pie, 117
Heaven, Chocolate, 117
Pecan Pie, Bourbon-
     Chocolate, 116
Chutney, Cranberry, 89
Coconut-Chocolate-Almond
     Cheesecake, 112
Coconut Joys, 147
Conserve, Caramelized Chicken
     with Cranberry, 80
Cookies
Bars and Squares
    Brownies, Chess, 133
    Cranberry-Caramel Bars, 132
    Hermits, 133
    Scotch Bars, Chewy, 134
Drop
    Almond Cookies, 126
    Chocolate Chip Cookies, Mom
         Ford's, 126
    Fruitcake Cookies, 128
    Oatmeal-Molasses
         Cookies, 128
Refrigerator
    Nutcracker Cookies, 131
    Pecan Crescent Cookies, 130

Shortbread, Brown Sugar, 130
Shortbread, Rum-Currant, 130
Thumbprints, Chocolate-
     Caramel, 127
Spritz Cookies, Christmas, 145
Corn
Muffins, Fiesta Corn, 39
Pudding, Dashiell Corn, 95
Salsa, Southwestern Black
     Bean-Corn, 141
Spoonbread, Corn, 37
Cornbreads
Dressing, Sweet Cornbread, 88
Fiesta Cornbread, 39
Sticks, Fiesta Corn, 39
Cornish Hens
Barley-Mushroom Stuffing,
     Cornish Hens with, 82
Orange-Ginger Hens with
     Cranberry Salsa, 81
Cranberries
Bars, Cranberry-Caramel, 132
Chutney, Cranberry, 89
Cider, Spiced Cranberry, 20
Conserve, Caramelized Chicken
     with Cranberry, 80
Oranges, Brandied Cranberry, 98
Relish, Tipsy Cranberry, 90
Salsa, Cranberry, 81
Vinaigrette, Cranberry, 101
Crêpes, Basic, 26
Crêpes, Sausage-Filled, 26

Desserts. See also Cakes, Candies,
     Cookies, Pies and Pastries.
Bombe, Double-Chocolate, 118
Cookies 'n' Cream
     Dessert, 123
Crème Brûlée, Black-and-
     White, 122
Flan, Pumpkin, 121
Ice Cream, Spiced, 115
Mousse, Chocolate, 118
Mousse, White Chocolate, 119
Tiramisu, 120
Trifle, Banana Pudding, 123
Dressing, Creole, 88
Dressing, Sweet Cornbread, 88
Dumplings, Chicken and, 57

Eggs
Casserole, Egg, 28
Grande, Eggs Oso, 25
Soufflé Roll, Southwestern, 24

Fish. *See also* Seafood.
  Snapper with Rosemary Sauce, 56
Frostings, Filling, and Toppings
  Apricot Glaze, 113
  Bourbon Glaze, Baked Ham
    with, 76
  Buttermilk Glaze, 106
  Cherry Glaze, 113
  Chocolate Ganache, 119
  Cream Cheese Filling, 141
  Cream Cheese Frosting, 106
  Cream Cheese Frosting,
    Nutty, 107
  Cream Cheese Frosting,
    Peppermint, 109
  Ice Cream Topping, Hot
    Fudge, 144
  Ice Cream Topping, Maple-
    Pecan, 145
  Oatmeal Cookie Topping, 97
  Peppermint Frosting option,
    Quick, 109
  Powdered Sugar Paints, 131
  Praline-Mustard Glaze, Apple-
    Stuffed Tenderloin with, 75
  White Chocolate-Buttercream
    Frosting, 111
Fruit. *See also* Apples, Apricot,
    Blackberry, Blueberry,
    Cherries, Coconut,
    Cranberries, Lemon,
    Oranges, Pear, Raspberry.
  Compote, Brandied Fruit, 29
  Compote with Caramel Syrup,
    Citrus, 29
  Cookies, Fruitcake, 128
  Punch, Sparkling Citrus, 21

Garnish
  Holiday Trees, 109
Gravies
  Redeye Gravy, Country Ham
    with, 26
  Sausage Gravy, 31
  Vidalia Onion and Giblet
    Gravy, 89
Grits, Garlic-Cheese, 28

Ham. *See also* Pork.
  Baked Ham with Bourbon
    Glaze, 76
  Country Ham with Redeye
    Gravy, 26
  Grilled Ham and Apples, 53

Jambalaya, 141
Melts, Ham and Cheese, 67
Soup, Ham 'n' Pot Liquor, 63

Jambalaya
  Jambalaya, 141
  Mix, Jambalaya, 141
  1-2-3 Jambalaya, 53

Lamb Sandwiches, 66
Lamb with Cherry-Wine Sauce,
    Hazelnut-Crusted Rack
    of, 73
Lemon
  Beef, Thai Lemon, 52
  Linguine, Lemon, 91
  Pie, Aunt Kitty's Lemon, 115
  Punch, Lemonade-
    Bourbon, 21

Mayonnaise, Raspberry, 66
Mincemeat Pie, Pear-, 114
Muffins
  Blueberry Streusel Muffins, 40
  Corn Muffins, Fiesta, 39
  Pecan-Orange Muffins, 40
Mushroom Stuffing, Cornish Hens
    with Barley-, 82
Mustard
  Dip, Sweet-and-Spicy
    Mustard, 8
  Glaze, Apple-Stuffed Tenderloin
    with Praline-Mustard, 75
  Sauce, Mustard, 75

Onions
  Oven-Roasted Potatoes, Green
    Beans, and Onions, 96
  Purple Onion, Spicy Green Beans
    with, 93
  Sauce, Beef Tenderloin with
    Five-Onion, 70
  Twist, Onion-Poppy Seed, 43
  Vidalia Onion and Giblet
    Gravy, 89
Oranges
  Cranberry Oranges, Brandied, 98
  Hens with Cranberry Salsa,
    Orange-Ginger, 81
  Muffins, Pecan-Orange, 40
  Turkey Breast, Rosemary-
    Orange, 59

Pancakes, German Potato, 37
Pasta
  Broccoli and Sausage, Pasta
    with, 54
  Fettuccine Supreme, Chicken, 57
  Linguine, Cracked Pepper, 91
  Linguine, Lemon, 91
  Shrimp, Spicy Pasta and, 56
  Spaghetti, All-in-One, 51
  Tortellini Tapas with Spicy
    Ranch Dip, 17
Peanut Clusters, 147
Peanut Fudge, Butterscotch-, 146
Pear-Mincemeat Pie, 114
Pear-Pecan Appetizers, 14
Pea Salad, Black-Eyed, 102
Pecans
  Appetizers, Pear-Pecan, 14
  Ball, Pinecone Cheese, 12
  Bread, Apricot-Pecan, 36
  Brownies, Chess, 133
  Cookies, Fruitcake, 128
  Cookies, Pecan Crescent, 130
  French Toast, Praline, 33
  Frosting, Nutty Cream
    Cheese, 107
  Logs, Caramel-Pecan, 135
  Millionaires, 135
  Muffins, Pecan-Orange, 40
  Pie, Bourbon-Chocolate
    Pecan, 116
  Pie, Mom's Pecan, 116
  Sugar-and-Spice Pecans, 8
  Topping, Maple-Pecan Ice
    Cream, 145
  Truffles, Chocolate-Praline, 136
Pepper Sauce, Red, 92
Pepper Spread, Roasted Red Bell, 11
Pies and Pastries
  Applesauce Pie, 115
  Bouchées aux Fruits de
    Mer, 78
  Brownie-Mint Pie, 117
  Burritos, Hot Phyllo, 16
  Chocolate Heaven, 117
  Lemon Pie, Aunt Kitty's, 115
  Pear-Mincemeat Pie, 114
  Pecan Pie, Bourbon-
    Chocolate, 116
  Pecan Pie, Mom's, 116
  Puffs, Savory Cheese, 16
Pork
  Chops with Black-and-White
    Salsa, Pork, 52
  Roast of Pork with Stuffing,
    Crown, 74

Tenderloin
    Grilled Pork Tenderloin,
        Molasses-, 53
    Medaillons in Mustard Sauce,
        Pork, 75
    Stuffed Tenderloin with Praline-
        Mustard Glaze, Apple-, 75
Potatoes. *See also* Sweet Potato.
    Hash Brown-Cheese Bake, 28
    Mashed Potato Bowls, 61
    Mashed Potatoes, Garlic-
        Gruyère, 96
    Oven-Roasted Potatoes, Green
        Beans, and Onions, 96
    Pancakes, German Potato, 37
    Salad, Greek Potato, 103
    Salad, Spicy Potato, 102
    Soup, Easy Potato-Sausage, 61
Pudding, Dashiell Corn, 95
Pumpkin Flan, 121

Quail with Red Wine-Blackberry
        Sauce, Grilled, 85

Raspberry-Cheese Coffee Cake, 30
Raspberry Mayonnaise, 66
Relish, Tipsy Cranberry, 90
Rice
    Holiday Rice, 90
    Red Beans and Rice, New
        Orleans, 54
    Risotto with Saffron,
        Pistachio, 91
    Salad, Waldorf Rice, 99
    Wild Rice-Stuffed Turkey
        Breast, 84
Rolls and Buns
    Cinnamon Rolls, Tiny, 32
    Sticky Buns, Christmas
        Morning, 33
    Yeast
        Cinnamon Rolls, 45
        Crescent Rolls, Make-
            Ahead, 47
        Herb Rolls, 45
        Refrigerator Yeast Rolls, 44
        Spoon Rolls, 46
        Sweet Potato Rolls, 45

Salad Dressings
    Basil Dressing, Spinach Salad
        with Feta Cheese and, 101
    Cranberry Vinaigrette, 101

Salads
    Black-Eyed Pea Salad, 102
    Cherry Salad, Congealed, 99
    Coleslaw, Best Barbecue, 102
    Greek Salad, Dawn's
        World-Famous, 103
    Green Holiday Salad with
        Cranberry Vinaigrette,
        Winter, 100
    Potato Salad, Greek, 103
    Potato Salad, Spicy, 102
    Rice Salad, Waldorf, 99
    Spinach Salad with Feta Cheese
        and Basil Dressing, 101
Salsas. *See also* Sauces.
    Black-and-White Salsa, Pork
        Chops with, 52
    Black Bean-Corn Salsa,
        Southwestern, 141
    Cranberry Salsa, 81
    Salsa, 24
Sandwiches
    Eggs Oso Grande, 25
    Ham and Cheese Melts, 67
    Lamb Sandwiches, 66
    Reubens, Oven-Grilled, 67
Sauces. *See also* Gravies, Salsas.
    Balsamic Sauce, 71
    Cherry-Wine Sauce, 73
    Chili Sauce, 143
    Mustard Sauce, 75
    Onion Sauce, Beef Tenderloin
        with Five-, 70
    Red Pepper Sauce, 92
    Red Wine-Blackberry Sauce,
        Grilled Quail with, 85
    Rosemary Sauce, Snapper
        with, 56
Sausage
    Crêpes, Sausage-Filled, 26
    Gravy, Sausage, 31
    Jambalaya, 1-2-3, 53
    Pasta with Broccoli and
        Sausage, 54
    Soup, Easy Potato-Sausage, 61
Seafood. *See also* Fish, Shrimp.
    Bouchées aux Fruits de Mer, 78
    Dressing, Creole, 88
    Spread, Grandma Reed's
        Seafood, 10
Shrimp
    Lafayette, Shrimp, 77
    Marinated Shrimp, 15
    Pasta and Shrimp, Spicy, 56
    Salad, Dawn's World-Famous
        Greek, 103

Slow Cooker
    Butter, Slow Cooker Apple, 143
    Red Beans and Rice, New
        Orleans, 54
Soufflé Roll, Southwestern, 24
Soufflés, Parmesan, 94
Soups. *See also* Chili, Jambalaya, Stew.
    Carrot-Butternut Squash Soup, 64
    Cheese Soup, Mexican, 64
    Chowder, Easy Vegetable, 65
    Ham 'n' Pot Liquor Soup, 63
    Potato-Sausage Soup, Easy, 61
    Turkey Soup, Tempting, 63
Spinach
    Dip in Sourdough Round,
        Spinach, 10
    Eggs Oso Grande, 25
    Salad with Feta Cheese and Basil
        Dressing, Spinach, 101
Squash Soup, Carrot-Butternut, 64
Stew, Make-Ahead Company
        Beef, 60
Stuffing, Cornish Hens with
        Barley-Mushroom, 82
Stuffing, Crown Roast of Pork
        with, 74
Sweet Potato-Eggnog Casserole, 97
Sweet Potato Rolls, 45

Tomatoes
    Dip, Layered Nacho, 9
    Salsa, 24
    Salsa, Pork Chops with
        Black-and-White, 52
    Sauce, Chili, 143
    Shrimp Lafayette, 77
    Spaghetti, All-in-One, 51
Turkey
    New Year's Turkey, 83
    Rosemary-Orange Turkey
        Breast, 59
    Soup, Tempting Turkey, 63
    Stuffed Turkey Breast, Wild
        Rice-, 84

Veal Chops, Herb-Peppered, 72
Vegetables. *See also* Asparagus,
        Broccoli, Brussels Sprouts,
        Corn, Mushroom, Onions,
        Pepper, Potatoes, Pumpkin,
        Squash, Sweet Potato,
        Tomatoes.
    Chowder, Easy Vegetable, 65
    Roasted Winter Vegetables, 97

Favorite Recipes Journal

Jot down your family's and your favorite recipes for quick and handy reference.
And don't forget to include the dishes that drew rave reviews when company came for dinner.

RECIPE	SOURCE/PAGE	REMARKS